MAKING THE MOST OF YOUR RESEARCH JOURNAL

Nicole Brown

First published in Great Britain in 2021 by

Policy Press, an imprint of
Bristol University Press
University of Bristol
1-9 Old Park Hill
Bristol
BS2 8BB
UK
t: +44 (0)117 954 5940
e: bup-info@bristol.ac.uk

Details of international sales and distribution partners are available at
policy.bristoluniversitypress.co.uk

British Library Cataloguing in Publication Data
A catalogue record for this book is available from the British Library

ISBN 978-1-4473-6004-9 paperback
ISBN 978-1-4473-6005-6 ePub
ISBN 978-1-4473-6006-3 ePdf

Cover design: Liam Roberts
Front cover image: Liam Roberts
Printed and bound by CPI Group (UK) Ltd, Croydon, CR0 4YY

To the most important, ever-supportive people in my
life, and the biggest fans anyone could have:
my two men Stephen and Craig,
my parents Seppi and Otti,
and my grandma Urla.

Contents

List of figures   vii
About the author   viii
Acknowledgements   ix
Foreword by Dannelle D. Stevens and Joanne E. Cooper   xii

How this book can help   1
    Chapter overviews   2

1   **Introducing research journals**   **3**
    Chapter aims   3
    Introduction   3
    Journals, logs, diaries or notebooks?   4
    What is research journalling?   6

2   **What does a research journal look like?**   **9**
    Chapter aims   9
    Introduction   9
    Choosing a research journal   11
    Choosing writing tools   14
    Choosing further materials   15
    Electronic journals   17
    Creating your research journal   21
    Try this!   23

3   **What to record in a research journal?**   **25**
    Chapter aims   25
    Introduction   25
    Note-taking as journalling   26
    Lists and schedules as journal entries   29
    Journalling from the field   35
    Practical journalling concerns   38
    Try this!   41

4   **How to record in a research journal?**   **43**
    Chapter aims   43
    Introduction   43
    Templates as journal entries   44
    Journalling with models of reflection   46

Fictionalisation and poetic inquiry   47
Playing with words   50
Making and doing as journal entries   52
Technology for journalling   55
Try this!   59

5   **When to record in a research journal?**   **61**
     Chapter aims   61
     Introduction   61
     Developing good habits   62
     Scheduling times for journalling   63
     From unscheduled to expected journalling   65
     Journalling means making choices   67
     Try this!   75

6   **What to do with the journal entries?**   **77**
     Chapter aims   77
     Introduction   77
     Using journal entries to provide evidence   78
     Making sense through journal entries   79
     From making sense to sharing   83
     Going back and forth   92
     Try this!   93

7   **Considerations of research journalling**   **95**
     Chapter aims   95
     Introduction   95
     Theoretical frameworks and the research journal   96
     Whose story, whose voice? The ethics of a research journal   101
     Pedagogy and the research journal   104

8   **Conclusion**   **107**
     The key messages   108

References   111
Index   127

List of figures

Full-size and full-colour versions of all the figures are available at https://policy.bristoluniversitypress.co.uk/making-the-most-of-your-research-journal/online-resources

2.1	Clare Daněk's stitch journal	22
3.1	Nicole Brown's sketchnote to accompany a presentation about STEP	28
3.2	Lesley Price's target tracker	31
3.3	Nicole Brown's finance tracker	32
3.4	Lauren Ackerman's research pipeline	34
3.5	Raul Pacheco-Vega's lecture notes	38
3.6	Raul Pacheco-Vega's to-do list	39
4.1	London School of Hygiene and Tropical Medicine's observation template	45
4.2	Aine McAllister's poetic inquiry	48
4.3	Nicole Brown's compete, compete, complete	50
4.4	Nicole Brown's word cloud	51
4.5	Madeline White's temperature scarf	54
5.1	Lesley Price's reading notes and annotations	68
5.2	Nicole Brown's vignette template	70
5.3	Nicole Brown's critical incident	71
5.4	Nicole Brown's application of a vignette template in a critical incident entry	72
6.1	Jason Wragg's sketch script page	85
6.2	Jason Wragg's page as completed by Innovative Pixels Art	86
6.3	Nicole Brown's COVID-19 fiction development	90
6.4	Nicole Brown's COVID-19 fiction scenes	91
8.1	Aine McAllister's journalling as a working mum	108

About the author

Dr Nicole Brown is an Associate Professor in Education at UCL Institute of Education and Director of Social Research & Practice and Education Ltd. Her research interests relate to physical and material representations and metaphors, the generation of knowledge and, more generally, research methods and approaches to explore identity and body work, as well as to advance learning and teaching within higher education. She combines teaching, research and activism with Practice As Research, which she writes about and teaches on. She has edited *Lived Experiences of Ableism in Academia: Strategies for Inclusion in Higher Education* (Policy Press, 2021) and *Ableism in Academia: Theorising Experiences of Disabilities and Chronic Illnesses in Higher Education* (UCL Press, 2020) and co-authored *Embodied Inquiry: Research Methods* (Bloomsbury, 2021).

Acknowledgements

In September 2015, I had been an academic for several years and had supervised a solid number of Master's-level (MA) students. As supervisor and mentor of MA-level dissertations and reports, I insisted my students maintain research journals to use them to great effect. The practice looked quite different from my theory. Students engaged in and with research were unsure and unclear about the role of the research log, and were worried about 'getting it right' rather than making the journal a useful tool for them. To be fair, throughout my own studies for an MA I had also kept a journal, which I had also not found particularly useful.

When I embarked on my own doctoral journey in September 2015, I wanted to start a journal that would be effective, reliable, appropriate and relevant. I was keen to ensure that my journal would contain all the information I would need, and that I would be able to make best use of my own entries. In short, I would have the journal of all journals.

I scoured university libraries, general libraries, specialist and non-specialist bookshops to find a guidebook that would help me achieve my aims. Unfortunately, I was not successful with that task. There was no such book. Consequently, I did what everyone does – I started maintaining a research journal in the format that I thought a research journal should have, using written entries in the form of what I thought a journal should look like.

As my engagement with creativity and imagination in research grew and took hold, I realised that my research journal did not work for me, so I started to experiment. In the subsequent years, I delivered sessions on creative research methods and started incorporating some of my ideas relating to research journals into the workshops. The feedback from workshop delegates and students was overwhelmingly positive, with many saying they felt that I had given them a 'licence' to do things differently, which positively impacted their reflective practices and their habits relating to maintaining a research journal. Having completed my PhD, I am now coming full circle with offering the book that I wanted to have and that I would have bought at the beginning of my journey.

I start by thanking those, whose fabulous contributions I was allowed to feature. I really enjoyed working with you all and having those conversations in all their shapes around what you do, why and how when you journal. Thank you Lesley Price, Aine McAllister, Lauren Ackerman, Raul Pacheco-Vega, Clare Daněk, Madeline White and Jason Wragg.

I would like to thank the postgraduate students from C5 to C9 of the Secondary Teacher Education Programme (STEP) at the UCL Institute of Education, whose struggle with journalling was a major impetus for me to develop appropriate resources and support materials.

Much encouragement for writing this book and sharing my resources has come from delegates at workshops and training events. I would therefore like to thank the Social Research Association and the National Centre for Research Methods as well as the participants in my creative methods and reflexivity workshops, for sticking with me and my crazy ways. In particular, I would like to thank Graham Farrant, Lindsay Adams, Graham Crow, Ros Edwards and Melanie Nind.

I have developed many of my ideas for journalling and workshop resources on the back of or in response to conversations. I would like to express my gratitude to my colleague-friends Amanda Ince, Rosalind Janssen, Jo Collins, Anjoom Mukadam and Sharmina Mawani. A special thank you to Aine McAllister, whose feedback on dipping in and out of drafts was motivating and helpful in shaping the book. Thank you also to Helen Kara, Inger Mewburn, Janet Salmons and Pat Thomson for the encouraging tweets, conference conversations and emails in support of this project.

I am particularly indebted to the playful and creative in my life, without whom I would not have been able to develop the confidence in sharing my creations. Thank you Nathalie Banaigs, Bob Lamoon, Lesley Samms, Max Kimber, Ruth Payne and Chris Blunkell, who are all affiliated to or members of Kent Creative (kentcreativearts.co.uk), Creek Creative (creek-creative.org) and/or the Pure Arts Group & Pure Arts Foundation (www.pureartsgroup.co.uk). And thank you Michelle Harris, Sabine Ganzer, Christa Glaser and Martina Ebner for inspiring, encouraging and challenging me in my creative endeavours.

Policy Press has been the perfect home for this book, and it was great to see my own enthusiasm reflected in the editors and associates. Thank you to Philippa Grand and Amelia Watts-Jones, to the anonymous reviewers, to the designers and to the copyeditor Dawn Rushen. It has been gratifying to see this book come to fruition due to your input.

Finally, I would like to thank my family for their unwavering support. Thank you Craig and Stephen, Oma and Opa, and Urla. I genuinely appreciate that you listened through my thinking-aloud to structure my work, that you celebrated with me the word-count milestones, and the things you did to take pressure off me, especially the cooking, obviously. In particular, I would like to express my gratitude to my husband Craig for his library. Although often a source of ridicule, it has proven rather invaluable.

Readers are invited to get in touch via my webpage (www.nicole-brown.co.uk) or on Twitter (@ncjbrown). Throughout the book the 🌐 icon indicates that there are either online resources or web pages for you to investigate further (please visit https://policy.bristoluniversitypress.co.uk/making-the-most-of-your-research-journal/online-resources).

Foreword

*Professor Dannelle D. Stevens
and Professor Joanne E. Cooper*

When we published our book on journal keeping in 2009, we included only one chapter and nine case studies on keeping a professional journal. Both of us were keeping professional journals, as well as personal ones, and had been making full use of this practice. What a delight to see that Nicole Brown has now elaborated the notion of keeping a professional journal into a focus on the research journal. She has written a practical book chock-full of useful ideas with permission to think broadly about what a research journal is and how you might use it. She urges you, the reader, to think beyond prescription about what a research journal should be to how this type of journal can be a positive practice in your professional life. She opens the door to keeping a research journal and invites you into a grand buffet of the many varied and nurturing possibilities for creating your own unique research journal.

For novice and even practised journal keepers, the big question is, just what does that journal look like? How do you choose what to record and when to record, and what to do with the journal entries when finished? Additionally, how do you approach research journal keeping with pleasure and excitement, and not as a dreaded task? How can you create a research journal that becomes essential and highly valued in your academic research and writing toolkit?

From workshops and consultations that we have given on journal keeping, we know that would-be journal keepers can be reluctant about starting because they may view themselves as failed journal keepers. They think back to the partially completed blank journals that are stuffed in a drawer or sitting on their bookshelves. Some realize that even the organisation software that they bought had such a steep learning curve that it was not worth the time to figure it out. Or they thought there was one perfect way to keep a journal and they haven't quite gotten themselves around to meeting their own expectations.

Over and over again in *Making the Most of Your Research Journal* Brown pulls the reader back from the cliff of despair and from being discouraged and overwhelmed. She provides a wealth of information about what research journal keeping choices are available, both digital and analogue, and how you might use the journal to track a research project, stay organised and remain enthused. Does she recommend one method? No, not at all. She shows you the myriad of possibilities, even down to the details such as the journal's shape, the type of paper, the kind of entries, the writing or drawing tools to use as well as computer interfaces. We particularly like her use of colour in handwritten journals. Some of you may love her suggestions for digital methods because the entries are then searchable, can be synced with other media and can include cut-and-pasted entries from elsewhere. This book is really about opening doors, not closing them, to find something that works for your purpose, your work and your personal preferences.

Brown underscores the additional benefits of a research journal keeping practice, such as developing your researcher identity and authorial voice. She emphasises a 'journalling mindset'. It is easy to define success in a particular way and then decide that you are a failure as you have not lived up to your expectations. Brown states, 'Success is journalling.' We agree. As long as the practice is working for you, you are a success. And the greatest pitfall to being successful is to define journalling too narrowly, and then to give up, when whatever you *think* you should be doing is not working. Try something else to spark your practice.

Brown has worked with many faculty members, scientists and artists who keep a research journal, and the book is full of photographs and descriptions of real journal pages, artefacts and drawings to ignite your imagination. In addition, she includes 'Try this' sections with concrete ways to experiment with her ideas.

Finally, as the heart and soul of journal keeping, Brown espouses a playful, expansive and creative view. Why would this approach be beneficial for you and your research? Essentially, your research reflects your response to the current literature in the field. Beyond that, your research and your writing reflect what you value, what you are passionate about and, basically, who you are. A research journal is not merely a mirror of your thinking, but also a sketchpad for taking risks, developing your voice and experimenting with fresh approaches. A research journal documents, expands and affirms your voice so that you can make a unique and authentic contribution to your discipline and to our scholarly conversations. Brown demonstrates the power of a research journal practice for the journal keeper's professional and personal life. We love her open attitude. She offers so many possibilities that no one could walk away saying, 'I have no idea how to do this.'

How this book can help

This book has been designed to provide practical guidance regarding how to keep a research journal and how to make the most of it. While as working documents research journals accompany the research process from initial conception through to dissemination, this book foregrounds journalling as integral to research. With this in mind, the book has been carefully structured to answer practical questions such as 'What should a journal look like?', 'What should I record and how?' and 'What do I do with the entries and notes?' At the same time, the book offers an overview of the use and relevance of research journals and provides an insight into theoretical frameworks, practical and ethical considerations that impact the process of maintaining research journals.

Each chapter focuses on practical ideas, techniques, strategies and tools related to research journalling. The guiding principle for the book is that you need to find out for yourself what works for you: from the choice of materials to be used for the journal and the format the journal takes through to the questions of how, when, where and why details are recorded, to finally, what to do with these notes and entries. Research journals and entries come in many different forms, and this book aims to present those as a stimulus, food for thought and examples to experiment with. Researchers, for whom the research journal is a helpful tool, have found their personal way of recording and maintaining details, and this book aims to show you that anything goes and is allowed. You are encouraged to engage with the book through your own journalling in response to the content presented in the chapters and by completing the tasks at the end of the chapters. The hope is that this will free you from the pressures you may experience regarding the aesthetics, correctness and applicability of research journals.

This book is aimed at new researchers, practitioner-researchers and anyone supporting new researchers and practitioner-researchers in the social sciences, humanities and allied subjects. It should provide impetus and support for researchers to consider roles and positionality within the research process, to *do* reflexivity in research journals, and to help bridge any perceived gaps between practice and research.

Chapter overviews

In Chapter 1, I introduce the concept of research journals in their historical development, and explore the context and relevance of research journalling as a basis for the subsequent practical chapters.

Chapter 2 deals with the question 'What does a research journal look like?' I present examples of journals that are commercially available or that can be created at home. Examples are evaluated for their strengths and weaknesses in relation to practical applications during the research.

Chapter 3 concerns 'What to record in a research journal?' I consider the research journal as a working document that helps us get and stay organised, as well as being a record of journalling from the field, which I present in the three major areas: observations and conversations, emotions and experiences, thoughts and reflections.

In Chapter 4, I use the categories and typologies presented in Chapter 3 to answer the question 'How to record in a research journal?' This chapter highlights that research journals do not necessarily have to follow any specific rules, and do not even have to be in written formats. I also outline the process of recording in relation to the choices that we make as researchers, thereby potentially overlooking important information.

Chapter 5 relates to 'When to record in a research journal?' I show that research journalling equates to good habits, but also to being prepared. I continue the theme of choices from Chapter 4, and highlight how to create the context for and justification of consistent note-taking. In doing so, I offer advice on and practical examples for how to deal with situations where we may have forgotten or missed something.

In Chapter 6, I focus on 'What to do with journal entries?' I consider the practicalities of revisiting the research journal and what we can learn from this process.

Chapter 7 is more theoretical in nature and returns to the threads woven into all the practical chapters. In this chapter, I demonstrate that research journalling is a valid research activity in itself, and I reflect on ethical matters and pedagogical considerations.

I use the Conclusion to reiterate the key messages from throughout the book that (1) anything and everything goes, (2) journalling must be fit for purpose and (3) journalling requires a specific attitude.

 Go to https://policy.bristoluniversitypress.co.uk/making-the-most-of-your-research-journal/online-resources for full-colour versions of the figures and online resources.

1

Introducing research journals

Chapter aims

- To introduce the context of research journalling.
- To provide the aims and purposes of research journals.
- To define research journalling for the scope of this book.

Introduction

Within the social sciences, anyone who has ever undertaken or been involved in research, or who has attended courses and workshops on research methods, will have been told about maintaining a research log, journal or diary. Research methods handbooks also mention logs, journals or diaries (see, for example, Hatch, 2002; Hahn, 2008; Shaw and Holland, 2014; Silverman, 2017; Forrester and Sullivan, 2018). Mostly, we are told to keep a journal to record our reflections on positionality for a reflexivity statement, our thought processes involved in narrowing down research topics, and to maintain our fieldnotes more generally. Yet, there is no specific guidance and support on how to keep an effective research diary, which notes to take, or what to do with our entries in a research journal. While research logs, like other forms of journalling, require regularity and consistency, in practice, many of us feel under pressure to produce entries that are also relevant and appropriate. Consequently, many of us give up on our research logs early on, only to realise later in our research journey that some notes or entries would or could have been useful.

This book does not claim to be exhaustive. Instead, it should be used as a stepping-stone towards making better use of research journals. With this book, I hope to inspire you regarding the form, format and content of a research journal, to experiment with less conventional approaches alongside more traditional paths. I hope to offer you the confidence you need to be able to trust your own instincts and to challenge and break free from existing paradigms and schools of thought. My hope is that you will realise there is nothing you *must* do, but that you have the freedom to do what *you* want in and with your research journal(s).

In this book, I argue that the reason why many of us are abandoning our research journals is not because we do not see the value in them, but because we have not found our own personal approach to maintaining them. So, right at the start of this book I kindly ask you to remain open-minded, to actively engage with the book and to get involved in the tasks set out at the end of the chapters. Let me introduce an analogy: If you were new to running, you would not expect to be able to run a full marathon on your first day of running. To successfully complete a marathon, you need many hours of deliberate and targeted training. Maintaining a research journal is not unlike preparing to run a marathon in that regular practice is required to take full effect. To continue this analogy, even with the best training, you will not break any marathon records if you were to put on a wetsuit and flippers – having and using the right tools are as important as the right training. Having said that, on the other hand, there are marathon runners specifically running for charity purposes and trying to gain sponsorships to support the charities of their choices. And some of them do so by wearing wetsuits and flippers. These runners in wetsuit and flippers may be breaking records regarding the number of sponsorships they gather or the time in which they secure those sponsorships. What I am trying to say is that ultimately the tool and the context need to fit the purpose. And this is where your open-mindedness is crucial. Some of the tasks presented in this book may appear unrelated to your particular discipline and to your specific context, topic, research project or research question. They have been included to encourage you to experiment, so that you will be able to identify the tools you are most comfortable with. At the same time, the book seeks to dispel the many myths of a perfect research journal, highlighting instead how different kinds of activities and purposes may be achieved with journalling.

I now outline the foundational principles of, and historical background to, maintaining journals to provide the grounding for the subsequent more practical chapters that follow.

Journals, logs, diaries or notebooks?

Journalling is neither new nor innovative, with the act of keeping records and providing commentaries for significant events dating back to ancient times. What we know about the realities of sociocultural life in Ancient Rome comes from reflections and commentaries meticulously recorded by figures such as Ovid, Marcus Aurelius or Tacitus alongside the *codices* (account books) and *commentariae* (chronicles) kept in most Roman households (Lejeune, 2009). Journalling then was a philosophical, spiritual or meditative act, political propaganda and social commentary, as well as a way of dealing with the mundane tasks of everyday life such as managing expenses. Unfortunately, despite some very prominent diaries, like those by Samuel Pepys, Anne Frank or Nelson Mandela, we seemed to have unlearned the many purposes of journalling over time.

However, with an increased interest in personal growth as well as professional development in an era when identity is fluid, flexible and mouldable, becoming a project of definition and self-definition (Giddens, 1991), journalling has made a comeback. In addition to the immediate benefits of improving learning and knowledge, developing writing skills and therefore supporting professional growth, journalling has undisputed advantages relating to personal wellbeing (Stevens and Cooper, 2009). There have never been more different categories of journals: learning journals; diaries; dream books or logs; autobiographies, life stories or memoirs; spiritual journals; professional journals; interactive reading logs; theory logs; and electronic journals (Hiemstra, 2001). In Euro-Western contexts, learning logs and reflective journals, especially within the discourses of professional learning, such as in education, nursing or medical training, have a long tradition dating back to John Dewey: 'to reflect is to look back over what has been done so as to extract the net meanings which are the capital stock of intelligent dealing with further experiences' (Dewey, 1938: 86).

The purpose of these professional logs or journals is twofold: they are a document to learn from and with, but they are also a formal record of learning (Wolf, 1996; Thomas, 1998; Costantino et al, 2002; Yoon et al, 2007). The concern with such learning logs and reflective journals, however, is that an individual's personal reflective practice is formally assessed (Hampton and Morrow, 2003). Thus, students who are trainee nurses or trainee teachers, for example, will be very careful about what they present in those logs or journals, and how (Mena-Marcos et al, 2013; Toom et al, 2015). Critiques of journals therefore focus specifically on their superficiality (Fook et al, 2006) and lack of theoretical engagement (Thompson and Pascal, 2012). Within creative disciplines such as the fine arts, music or creative writing, by contrast, logs, journals or sketchbooks play a somewhat different role, in that they provide a safe space to play and experiment, to try out, design and fine-tune ideas (Delacruz and Bales, 2010; Heller and Landers, 2014a, b; Dabner et al, 2017; Sorger and Udale, 2017). Although journals and sketchbooks are sometimes also evaluated and assessed as part of university courses in the creative disciplines, they are designed in such a way that they instil good, regular habits of working in and on the journals and logs, as they are an intrinsic part to the process of being creative.

Given the wide variety of uses of diaries, notebooks, journals and logs in many different disciplines, we must ask ourselves if there can ever be one key understanding of what is or makes a research journal as well as if there is any reason for looking outside our own disciplines at all. Rather than seeing the many varieties and options as overwhelming and irrelevant, I would like to actively use them here because I think we can all learn from one another. Many researchers abandon their journals because they feel uncomfortable with the process, only to come to regret that decision later on. If, however, we are able to draw on different disciplinary conventions, to try out ideas that work elsewhere, then maybe we will find it within ourselves to maintain the habit and practice of journalling. As such, an artist's sketchbook is a helpful example of a research journal in social sciences, or the record of an archaeological dig is a useful example of recording factual information in history research. For the purposes of this book, then, what is research journalling?

What is research journalling?

Language is ambiguous and arbitrary. Consequently, terms that appear clear-cut and well defined are actually not. This is also true for research journals. As a teacher, teacher–educator, teacher–researcher and sociologist I regularly use the terms 'journal', 'log' and 'portfolio' for their specific meanings. Within teacher education a 'portfolio' would be a selection of works to demonstrate how the teacher meets specific professional criteria to be awarded a teaching qualification, whereas in sociology a portfolio is more loosely interpreted and signifies a collection of relevant pieces of works. Similarly, a research log could be a factual record of results or evidence and documentation of reflective practice.

The difficulty around terminology is particularly well expressed in Louise Fluk's (2009, 2015) reviews that have identified more than 30 terms to describe what I refer to as 'professional learning logs' and what she describes as 'narratives of research': a pedagogic strategy and an evaluation tool (Fluk, 2009: 40). However, it is not the terminology on its own that concerns us here. With the different descriptions and uses of words come divergent interpretations and applications. Logs, for example, tend to be seen as more descriptive and factual than journals. The use of the term 'journal', in turn, implies that the records are added to on a regular, even daily, basis (Fluk, 2009). As a result, the scope of journalling and logging ranges from listing results (Bolner et al, 2013), responses to guide questions (Lacy and Chen, 2013) and note-taking in two columns (Ballenger, 2014) to more detailed reflections in prose (Bonnet et al, 2013; Bruno and Dell'Aversana, 2017). Within professional learning contexts, the reflections in prose and the responses to guide questions are also combined in tasks that require learners to create journal entries based on their application of a particular reflective model, such as those by Rolfe et al (2001), Brookfield (1995), Gibbs (1988) or Kolb (1984).

I hope to debunk the many myths surrounding research journals, and so I deliberately use the term 'journalling' when describing the process of creating an entry in a research journal. Research entries may be reflections written in prose, but if we are looking to other disciplines and contexts, the process of journalling does not necessarily entail words at all. Art journalling, for example, is the process of keeping a visual diary that allows the journaller 'to examine, to challenge, to remember, to dream' (Ludwig, 2011a: 12). The purpose of art journalling is not necessarily to develop work or ideas, but to record what happens in the moment, as a form of commentary or memory-making and memory-keeping. In this sense, the process of art journalling is reflective, as the journaller is trying to get closer to their own experiences in order to then express and communicate them in a visual form of sketches, paintings, photographs and collages (Ludwig, 2011b). It is this reflective nature of art journalling that is actively employed and commented on in the contexts of art therapy, the arts as therapeutic interventions and arts education (Deaver and McAuliffe, 2009; Beaumont, 2012; Rubin, 2016; Gibson, 2018). Art journalling or visual journalling sits alongside other kinds of journalling, storytelling and narrative approaches to support therapy or counselling (Parker and Wampler, 2006; Bjorøy et al, 2016; Lindahl, 2018).

Even though seasoned journallers talk about the therapeutic and cathartic properties of journalling, journalling does not need to be therapeutic in its intention. It may simply be an act of meditation. In art journalling, the meditative effect comes to play when the journaller lets themselves be guided by the process of creation and follows the natural, intuitive flow of the arts. From the early 2000s, there has been a significant rise in interest in journalling for meditative purposes, with themed journals having gained significant popularity. There are now gratitude journals, dream journals, prayer journals and future journals, all of which follow specific prompt templates and stimulus for creating entries. A particularly successful venture is the bullet journal, as invented and advocated by the US author and designer Ryder Carroll. The bullet journal is a tool to develop good habits of mindfulness for an intentional life that is productive and effective, but also brings joy and pleasure (Carroll, 2018). Bullet journalling is a specific approach to reflect on, capture and make sense of the past, to provide targeted support for tasks in the present, and to create action plans towards future goals and achievements.

In short, journalling is a way of thinking through making, doing, creating and recording for the purpose of self-discovery, mindfulness, personal development and productivity. As for the research journal, it may be helpful to frame the journalling process in a similar way: research journalling, then, is a way of thinking through making, doing, creating and recording for the purpose of discovery, grounding, professional development and productivity. With this in mind, let us now consider in detail what a research journal looks like, what to record, how and when to record, and what to do with the journal entries to make the most of research journalling and the research journal.

2

What does a research journal look like?

Chapter aims

- To outline some of the many options available for journalling.

- To introduce the idea of using different or new materials and tools for journalling.

- To support decision-making by considering the advantages and drawbacks of individual approaches.

Introduction

What a research journal looks like depends on what, when and how you want to record your entries. This chapter should therefore stand alongside or after Chapters 3, 4 and 5. However, this chapter stands early in the book because most often our first thought relating to maintaining a research journal is to choose the right tools, and thus, to buy the right journal.

This assumption about the right research journal points to an important myth, namely that there is *the* research journal. In reality, we rarely get to see each other's research journals, but when we do, our misconceptions may be skewed further. I myself have attended conferences or workshops where I ended up sitting next to the person with *the* research journal: a perfect, pristine, beautiful, well-organised, hand-paginated book with cross-references and annotations, containing key words and search terms along with an index, and all in perfect cursive handwriting. My own scribbles across several loose, unnumbered pages not only pale in comparison, but become a source of deep embarrassment, guilt and envy in those moments. What I have learned over the years is that for many academics *the* research journal they bring to conferences or workshops is not their only one, and that their *other* research journals look quite different.

Reading through research reports, journal articles and other publications relating to research processes, we are consistently confronted with outputs that claim excellence, originality, perfection and success. As researchers we all know that research is messy, chaotic, untidy, disorderly. Yet publications hardly ever account for this nature of research. Consequently, we are led to believe that research processes are smooth, consistent, coherent and faultless. Although consciously we are aware that in disseminating research difficulties and messiness are glossed over, we are still impacted by and drawn to perfection and excellence. As the research journal accompanies the research process and is hardly ever shared within the dissemination of findings, we fall prey to the myth that the research journal itself is also pristine and excellent.

In my experience as a researcher, but also from teaching and delivering workshops, I regularly notice that many of us engaged in and with research are unsure and unclear about the role of the research journal, are worried about 'getting it right' and work on *the* research journal rather than creating a useful tool. Publications aiming to support researchers with maintaining a journal do not necessarily help either. These journal templates and guidebooks are well meaning in that they provide prompts for thoughts and ideas for what to record (Crown Journals, 2019; Bassot, 2020), but they are often framed or presented as accompanying a smooth research journey, as if journalling were a targeted, focused task. I appreciate the contributions these publications make in helping novice researchers develop good habits in journalling; I am only concerned that they perpetuate existing myths around *the* research journal.

Publications relating to fieldnotes and maintaining records, particularly in ethnographic contexts, have a different, but equally intimidating, effect as advice and guidance are framed as 'should and should not' statements (Emerson et al, 2011; Atkinson, 2020). Again, I do not deny the wealth of learning I myself have gained from carefully reading and rereading how to record fieldnotes and write ethnographically. However, the message from such publications is clear: *the* research journal is a book with notes written into it. It goes without saying that writing helps make sense of experiences and will support analytical processes. In reality, however, the written form is not the only form or mode of communication. So we should ask ourselves why a research journal should be limited to that particular form or shape of a notebook.

What follows on from here is a presentation of tools for research journals. Some of the examples are commercially available while others will need to be created at home. In the course of this, I outline the advantages, drawbacks, strengths and weaknesses in relation to the practical applications during the research. This leads back to the analogy of the marathon runner wanting to break speed records and the marathon runner in the wetsuit seeking to gain sponsorship, as not every option is suited for each purpose.

Choosing a research journal

There are many notebooks, journals, diaries and planners commercially available – from cheap exercise books and notepads to expensive, themed diaries with cloth or leather binding and locket closures.

Depending on what you would like to record in your journal, when and how (see Chapters 3, 4 and 5), you may decide to have several journals in different sizes and formats, or you may prefer one particular shape and paper type, and buy several copies of that same book to use for all of your purposes, or you may even have only one chosen format to work in. There is no rule. We should just remind ourselves that there is not *the* research journal. A research journal is meant to be a tool to support the research process and to make academic life easier. The aim, therefore, is to find what works for you.

At the time of writing, my physical 'research journal' is a collection of 12 different notebooks and pads as well as four ring binders, with each having its own particular purpose. For the sake of full disclosure: these notebooks and pads sit alongside electronic records on my desktop computer and 50-odd other physical versions that have been fully or partially completed, or entirely abandoned.

Format and size

The market is saturated with planners and notebooks in all formats and sizes. The most common formats are landscape, portrait or square, and the most common paper sizes are A4, B5, A5, B6 and A6. The numbers of pages in a notebook should also be considered as part of the format and size, as these will determine the thickness of the pad or book. With so many options available it is difficult to see which one is right, and it may well be that you need to try several before you can identify your preferred version. This is one of the reasons why I have so many partially completed or abandoned journals.

Smaller, thinner notebooks and pads are easier to put into pockets and bags. You are more likely to have these with you when you go out for a walk or shopping. Therefore, you will probably use them more often and consistently than thicker, bigger, expensive notebooks or journals. The advantage of these larger formats is that you can have all of your entries in one place rather than having them spread across several smaller pads. If you are taking pride in your notes, larger, expensive formats may also be more attractive for you.

Considering note-taking, larger formats allow you to break the pages into columns, which smaller formats do not. For example, you may want to have a page for reading notes and leave space for your annotations later on. With A4 pages, you can fold over part of the page to create a two-third to one-third split. The two-third column will give you plenty of space for your reading notes; the one-third column offers enough space for annotations.

The most interesting formats and shapes come from artistic conventions with concertina-style notebooks, where pages are folded in an accordion or zigzag. In a notebook you have the original size, like an A5 page, but you are then able to open up that page to three or four times the width. The advantage of this is that you have a long panorama format in front of you, which is perfect for workflow diagrams and sketches. The disadvantages are that the folds may be distracting and that the pages open up over the edge of a book, which may make it difficult for you to work on, unless you have some other books or notepads you can put underneath to level the working surface.

Bindings and covers

Bindings and covers of notebooks and pads should be considered in as much detail as their format and size. You need to weigh up the protection and longevity of a notebook or pad against its practicability and flexibility. Hardbound books will provide more protection and so your journal will be more long-lived, but pads with soft bindings will be easier to slip into pockets and bags. The commercially available hardbound copies sometimes include extras, which may or may not be a decisive factor for you. Elasticated ribbons as a closure system, ribbon bookmarks and pouches for small souvenirs or tickets are the most commonly incorporated accessories.

Equally, whether pages are perforated to be torn out, hole-punched or tightly bound into the notebook will have a bearing. The advantage of hole-punched, tear-out pages is at the same time their disadvantage. Taking pages out of a notebook may help you with organising your research journal according to the themes or topics you are covering, but the perforation obviously weakens the pages to such an extent that they may fall out.

Bindings and covers also have an impact on how you work. Some hardbound books are so tightly bound that it is very difficult to lay the book out completely flat. Ring or spiral bindings can be laid flat, but in portrait-sized books the rings will be in your way as you are working over the spiral or rings. In this case, a book that is spiral bound on the short side for a landscape format may be more suitable.

One thing to bear in mind is that there is always an opportunity to experiment with pages. For example, if you have an A4 notebook that is spiral bound on the long side, you do not necessarily have to use it in the intended portrait format. Maybe sometimes, or even always, you could turn your notebook around so that the page becomes landscape. Again, there is no rule that says that a portrait page has to be used as a portrait page.

I know that the formatting of the covers leads us into a particular way of thinking. If that is bothering you, you can create your own cover over the existing one. For many of my own journals, I have created two cover pages, one at the front and one at the flipped-over back. This means I have effectively created two front pages and can work my way from the front to the middle section of the notebooks for two different reasons or projects.

Paper weight

Paper weight is indicated as grams per square metre (GSM or g/m^2), which stands for the weight of a fabric or paper if you take one sheet of 1 metre by 1 metre in size. The grams per square metre value therefore indicate how heavy or light a sheet of paper is, whereby the weight of the paper directly corresponds to the thickness of a page. A higher grams per square metre value signifies a much thicker page, with standard pages tending to be around $80g/m^2$. There is again no right or wrong regarding paper weight, only suitability for a task. For jotting notes in a journal using a pencil or biro, $80g/m^2$ paper will be perfect. If you would like to use ink or sharpie pens, for example, the writing will shine through, as the paper is too thin. Art sketchbooks intended for use with watercolours are often around $200g/m^2$, with mixed media sketchbooks being sold at $300g/m^2$. A notebook of 32 sheets at $300g/m^2$ is practically as thick as a notebook with 70 sheets of $90g/m^2$ paper.

The thicker a page is in a notepad, the more expensive the pad becomes, but the more choices you have for which media you are working with. Sticking and gluing, painting and water washing all put a strain on the paper, and if the paper is not thick enough, it will not hold. However, even thicker paper may buckle and bend, making the journal bigger and more unwieldy.

Page patterns

Blank, ruled or lined, squared or grid, dotted, with or without margins – these are only some choices that are on offer. There are also planners with pre-printed dates, weeks or months spread over one or two pages to account for 12 or 18 months. And then there are the themed pre-printed journals, such as travel journals, reading logs and book journals aimed at recording or tracking experiences and memories, with each brand of journal having its own layout and feel. Again, with so many patterns on offer, it is not surprising that we can feel overwhelmed when faced with making a choice.

The main consideration in selecting a page pattern is about your personal preference. Blank pages do not have any guiding lines, which may make handwriting more difficult, but open the page up to more creative ways of working. The lines are helpful for keeping any text straight and steady, but may, in turn, stifle the creativity the blank page affords. Of course, having a ruled page does not mean it is impossible to sketch; it just means that there are lines, which feel distracting or intrusive, making the final page 'untidy'. By contrast, the grid pages are helpful for developing architectural and design sketches or graphs. Most recently, journals with dotted pages have become particularly popular, as the dots offer some guidelines for writing texts or drawing sketches to support neatness, tidiness and structure, but are not as intrusive as full lines or grids, thus offering some freedom and creativity.

Choosing writing tools

Pens and biros, pencils and brushes are all writing tools and mark-making implements. As the format, size, bindings and covers, paper weights and page patterns impact on our ways of working, so, too, is our journalling affected by the mark-making tools in our hands. The important factor here is to have the right implement or tool for the given purpose.

If you have a journal with thin paper, then using paint brushes and ink will be difficult because the text will shine through to the next page, and the one after that. At the same time, the writing tool should feel comfortable in your hand. Brushes and calligraphy pens encourage creativity and following the flow of the medium, but are not as conducive to making copious notes.

Pencils, pens, markers and biros

Pencils, pens, markers and biros can be the cheapest options for writing, although there are ranges in prices depending on brands, sizes and uses. There are thin, small pencils, as well as thick-grip pens. Pens and markers may have the finest points as tips or can produce chunky lines with thick tips. Some inks are water soluble; others are not. Pencils and some ink pens allow for erasing, whereas biros or felt-tip pens tend not to. Graphite pencils are available in different scales of hardness, from the hardest, lightest 9H pencil to the softest, darkest 9B pencil, with the most commonly used HB pencil in the middle of the range. Similarly, fountain pen tips may have a harder or softer feel when writing.

As always, there are trade-offs. Markers with chunky tips may not be as helpful when trying to write individual words or record details in a sketch but will have better coverage for mark-making. Thin lines from fine-lined pencils, by contrast, leave space for details later, but require that detail to make an impact. Inks that are not water soluble can be used for more creative kinds of works alongside paints and watercolours, whereas ink pens and harder pencils will disappear against those. Marks made with softer graphite pencils, however, may smudge and rub off, unless you use a fixative on the page.

Choosing further materials

There is no rule that restricts the research journal to black writing on a white background. In fact, it is not the research journal or journalling that stifles our creativity and imagination, but our own limited view of what constitutes a research journal. Instead of perpetuating existing ideas regarding what a research journal looks like, we should experiment to find what feels most comfortable and suitable for us. Introducing colour and/or textures to a research journal allows for a veritable wealth of possibilities, from highlighting and emphasising to expressing and communicating.

Coloured pencils, paints, watercolours and brushes

Coloured pencils and coloured highlighter pens are available cheaply and a few selected pencils in blue, red and yellow or highlighter pens in yellow, pink, orange and green can be carried around easily, too. Although coloured pencils are reminders of children's colouring books for many people, using them allows you to capture moods and impressions quickly and effectively without the need for any additional materials or resources. There are also water-soluble coloured pencils, which can be used with brushes, to create interesting watercolour effects and enable smoother blending between colours. To limit the number of tools that need to be carried around, there are waterbrushes. A waterbrush looks like a pen that has a water reservoir with a brush tip, so it is effectively a brush in the shape of a pen.

Watercolour sets and brushes represent another step up in the creative toolkit. Many artists use sets of six or twelve watercolour pans along with different kinds of watercolour brushes. There is an abundance of arts materials, from watercolour sets with cheaper synthetic brushes through to expensive branded watercolour pans and brushes made of natural hair. As with pencils and pens, the brushes, too, come in differently sized handles and brush tips, and again, the choice of what is right lies with how comfortable the brush and its sweep feel. Watercolours are particularly suited to expressively capturing moods and impressions in the moment, but do require heavier paper and water, which makes them less conducive to carrying around.

Pastels and acrylics

Pastels are sticks of pigment and binding materials that are sold in several forms. The most commonly used pastels are hard or soft. Hard pastels contain less pigment and are therefore more useful as a tool for drawing or fine-tuning details. Soft pastels contain higher levels of pigment, which makes them easier to blend and smudge on paper, but also creates more dust. Because of their soft property, colour blending on paper can be done with your fingers or a soft cloth. The soft pastels are therefore particularly helpful in capturing shades of colours. However, the finished page will need to be protected, for example with a fixative, to avoid unwanted smudging.

Acrylics are fast-drying paints that are water soluble initially but become water resistant when they are dry. This means that working with acrylics makes it possible to replicate the feel and texture of watercolours as well as of oil paints by regulating how much water is used during painting. Once the acrylics have dried, the paint is considered as non-removable, although there are ways to lift some fresh paint layers off with isopropyl alcohol. The advantage of acrylics lies with their flexibility to enable the effects of watercolours or oil paintings, but their major disadvantages are drying time and the fact that you will need some work surface rather than being able to use them when you are out and about.

Mixed-media tools

Once we allow creativity to unleash, it becomes evident that there are so many more options available. As there is no rule about the research journal and regarding journalling, there is also no limit to opportunities. For example, you may want to create collages as expressions of your experiences or analyses (see Chapters 3 and 6). To this end, you could collect artefacts from your walks, snippets from magazines or other printed pages along with samples of fabrics or ribbons. Working these materials into a collage means that you will require a good pair of scissors, solid adhesives like glue and glue sticks, adhesive tape, some paints for developing a background, pens to add fine details, and so on. You could also experiment with materials like clay, Plasticine, sand or jewellery-making wires. The advantages of mixed-media techniques are that the processes and the products are expressive as well as emotive, and therefore help people connect emotionally and viscerally. The drawbacks of this kind of work are that these processes are time-consuming and that you require physical, intellectual and mental space to engage in these creative processes.

Electronic journals

With the widespread use of electronic gadgets, smartphones and tablets alongside the continuous development of computers and laptops, keeping records of experiences has changed drastically. We can now take and share photographs, videos or audio recordings readily at any time. Indeed, sharing our recordings has become part of our routine that is shaping our personal as well as our professional life. In the context of research journals, we can build on our everyday routines and behaviours and draw on those for the purpose of journalling.

The basic principle that there are no rules or limits around the research journal also applies here. For some of us, it feels so natural to write text documents and emails, or to maintain a website or an electronic diary, that it would be only 'right' to maintain the research journal electronically, too. Indeed, blog posts on personal and professional websites along with social media messages should be considered as valuable entries to the research journal (more about this in Chapter 3).

Text documents

The creation of text documents is probably the simplest form of electronic journalling. However, as Graham Greene so aptly highlights, there is something about typing that does not compare to handwritten work:

> My two fingers on a typewriter have never connected with my brain. My hand on a pen does. A fountain pen, of course. Ball-point pens are only good for filling out forms on a plane. (Graham Greene, writing in the *International Herald Tribune*, 7 October 1977)

Using a pen and feeling the movement and flow on paper are themselves intuitive, emotive and creative acts and experiences. Additionally, with the way that word processing allows for deleting, inserting, cutting and pasting, the process of putting words on paper is perhaps not as deliberate, considered and careful. As a result, handwritten journal entries may be better at capturing the raw, authentic and immediate, while electronic entries come across as more distant.

However, electronic entries to research journals have huge advantages over handwritten journals: documents are searchable and can be shared easily, texts can be directly lifted and moved through cutting and pasting, annotations can be added at any time with no concern for space to be limited. Smartphones, tablets and laptops can be synced with one another so that the entries can be accessed from anywhere at any time, making them proper working documents. For research entries as text documents to be particularly useful tools, it is best to have a clear system of saving and tagging documents and to ensure regular backups across several machines, platforms or external storage devices. And if an entry is unusually important, there is always the option to print the page, so that the paper copy can be retyped, if the worst comes to the worst.

Multimedia research entries

Another major benefit of electronic journals is the opportunity to incorporate different kinds of records either via a link to a web page or via embedding photographs, videos and audio recordings. Word processing programs are able to do that to a particular extent, but specific applications and software are available for such purposes. While new users will need to learn to find their way around the systems on offer, applications and software can support the process of journalling quite significantly. It would be impossible for me to review all of the different options on the market, especially as the market is so fast-paced, with applications and software constantly appearing and disappearing. But this book would not be complete if we did not consider some of the most commonly used applications and programs, their purposes and potential for research journals.

Note-taking and information-sharing programs

Microsoft OneNote is a note-taking program that encourages the free-form collection, recording and sharing of information. There is no particular structure or layout to the page, and it can save notes that are handwritten on tablets with stylus pens as well as videos, photographs and text documents. OneNote enables you to collate information from different sources, to gather that information in one place and to annotate and add to it as required. The fact that there is no structure or layout to the page means that page sizes become arbitrarily large. Another issue is the reliance on technology syncing and connecting appropriately, which may cause problems at times when trying to embed different file types. Although OneNote is probably the market leader for information collection and sharing, there are significantly successful alternatives available, such as Evernote, Google Keep and Wunderlist, for example. The advantages and disadvantages of those programs lie in their ranges of functionalities, options for storage, access to an account or development for different operating systems. Google Keep and Wunderlist emphasise workflow and task management by focusing on functions and processes related to to-do lists, whereas Evernote emphasises multimediality, compatibility and searchability. Google Keep and Wunderlist may therefore be more suitable for spontaneous note-taking, whereas Evernote is conceptualised as a tool to support making and keeping memories.

Referencing software and applications

Different kinds of programs and applications are available for keeping records of readings for the purposes of building a bibliography. As the market moves quickly it is always worth keeping an eye out for new developments in that field, as the functions and options vary between the programs. The basic principle for all of the referencing programs, however, is to record the metadata of publications, so that on the click of a few buttons a bibliography can be produced in different referencing styles. The most commonly available, most widely used and, to date, longest living referencing programs are Zotero, Mendeley, EndNote and RefWorks (for more information see, for example, Butros and Taylor, 2010; Hensley, 2011; Marino, 2012; Ray and Ramesh, 2017;

Ivey and Crum, 2018). Again, new users will need to learn to use the software package and will be required to pay for licences, which may influence which of the programs are chosen. It is, of course, possible to maintain these reading records manually in a Word document, but the programs available have significant advantages, of which the creation of a bibliography in any referencing style is only one. The programs suggest articles similar to the ones in your existing datasets, thereby helping you identify what you should be reading and expanding your horizon. Datasets from the referencing programs can be exported and imported, so that sharing references becomes easy. Zotero, Mendeley and RefWorks are set up to support collaboration and social networking, but EndNote can even match a manuscript to a potential journal, thereby supporting the publications processes significantly. Ways of working also differ somewhat between the tools, as RefWorks is purely web-based, for example, whereas references can be saved locally on your computer for offline working with Zotero, Mendeley and EndNote. By contrast, mobile app versions of these programs are only available for Mendeley and, in the case of EndNote, just for iPads. Zotero and RefWorks function as mobile-friendly sites, but do not run as mobile apps.

Blogs, vlogs, podcasts and social media accounts

We often share content, experiences and reflections via social media accounts, blogs, podcasts and/or vlogs. The 'what to record' is covered in Chapter 3, but let it be said here that blog posts, video messages and social media postings are valuable platforms and tools for the purposes of research journalling. The choices are boundless, with the most commonly used platforms being Facebook, Twitter, Instagram, Pinterest, YouTube and Vimeo, alongside any web space using website builders such as Wix, WordPress or Squarespace. The focus on what is being communicated, how and why varies. For example, the limitation of 280 characters on Twitter makes it more difficult to communicate complex issues, and may only work in conjunction with a YouTube channel or WordPress page. By contrast, the more static surface of a WordPress or Wix page will not be as conducive to building a network of like-minded scholars for the exchange of ideas and constructive feedback, which Facebook offers.

Which platforms or tools should be used depends on personal preferences as well as disciplinary conventions. The main advantage of research journalling using these platforms could potentially be its main disadvantage: the option to share content more widely. It is not unknown in academia that ideas get taken without attributions (see Gadd et al, 2003a, b, c; Clarke, 2006; Bretag and Mahmud, 2009). Sharing information via the internet therefore requires considerable thought to balance the benefits against the potential drawbacks. However, social media and web spaces allow for building a narrative of research or a trajectory of a research career, which enables us to position ourselves in an increasingly competitive environment.

Creating your research journal

Coming to the end of this chapter, it should be obvious that there is not one research journal and that there are many options for what a research journal may look like. Initially, it is all about making choices about what to record, when and how, which will have an impact on the design or style of your research journal.

The following photograph (see Figure 2.1) is an example from Clare Daněk, who uses autoethnographic methods to explore how people learn amateur craft skills together in community making spaces. For two years, Clare used a stitch journal as a practical route to reflexivity and an opportunity to do some making every day.

For Clare, stitching offered a helpful and liberating tool for thinking through things and expressing herself visually and materially, without having to think about constructing arguments or synthesis or any of the complexities of more traditional academic forms. Throughout the process, Clare also shared the entries via her website (https://claredanek.me/stitch-journal), which are now a record of what each square means.

Not everyone will feel equally comfortable with stitching, but there are plenty of other opportunities to create journals. You could try Plasticine or clay for sculpting, or LEGO® or other children's toys. You could combine a physical moleskin-type journal with electronic journalling through a blog, or have a ring binder with loose pieces of paper to include thicker paper for more artistic expressions in addition to plain white pages of writing. While you are still experimenting with different shapes, formats and media, I recommend you have one index page where you make a note of what you have recorded or saved where. As you develop your own unique way of journalling, you will develop a system that is meaningful for you, and this index will become superfluous. Until then, you will want to make sure you can find your entries again.

Figure 2.1: Clare Daněk's stitch journal

TRY THIS!

Create your own journals and journal pages

The purpose of this chapter was to highlight that there is no one perfect or correct journal. These end-of-chapter tasks are therefore asking you to experiment with different forms and formats.

Create and use an 'annotations' page

Use an A4-sized lined piece of paper. On the long edge, fold it over at approximately 7 cm, then open the page again. You now have a page with a two-third to one-third split. The next time you are recording reading or meeting notes, use this annotations page to see what it feels like. Initially, using two-thirds of the page only may feel like a waste of paper, but once you revisit that page, you may start to feel differently. See the online resources for a video of how to create the annotations page (https://policy.bristoluniversitypress.co.uk/making-the-most-of-your-research-journal/online-resources).

Make your own mini-journal

Use one piece of paper of any size and fold it in half along the long edge, then that narrow edge into half and half again. You now have eights. Unfold the paper and fold along the short edge and using a pair of scissors, cut along the middle line closest to you through the first section. Unfold the paper, now fold along the long edge and collapse all pages into a small book. Flatten the page and then staple to secure the pages. Take this mini-journal with you the next time you are going for a walk, and experiment with sketching and jotting. See the online resources for a video of how to create the mini-journal (https://policy.bristoluniversitypress.co.uk/making-the-most-of-your-research-journal/online-resources).

Experiment with paper

Building on the idea of 'junk journals', use different types of papers to create your own journal. Search the internet for 'junk journals' for instructions on how to bind the papers together. Next time you are recording notes, use some of the pages in the junk journal to see how you feel about using this type of journal.

Check out online research journals

Many scholars maintain websites and blogs, and entries on those pages most often relate to their research and teaching work. Without knowing the contexts and circumstances of other academics, many entries can still very clearly be identified as coming out of and linking to research projects and individuals making sense of their own experiences. As a starting point I would recommend browsing the websites listed below. Most of these have been maintained for quite a while and are unlikely to disappear any time soon, but also, the academics behind them are very active on social media such as Twitter, YouTube and Facebook:

- Nadine Muller: http://nadinemuller.org
- Helen Kara: https://helenkara.com
- Pat Thomson: https://patthomson.net
- Inger Mewburn: https://thesiswhisperer.com
- Tara Brabazon: https://brabazon.net
- Raul Pacheco-Vega: www.raulpacheco.org

3

What to record in a research journal?

Chapter aims

- To outline the scope of research journalling.

- To introduce particular ways of recording for specific purposes.

- To consider research journalling in its practicalities, with all its consequences.

Introduction

As outlined in Chapter 1, the contents of journal entries depend on the overall purpose of the research journal, as the journal may be linked to professional development, qualifications and assessments. Within research handbooks, the outline of what to record is often limited to vague guidance relating to making fieldnotes and recording observations, for example. In reality, the choice of what must be recorded, should be noted or is written down is much more complex. We have all been in situations where we have had to ask ourselves if our thoughts or observations were actually relevant enough, or where we had had a conversation that was not strictly a fieldwork conversation, but that seemed important nonetheless. So should we then write an entry about that non-fieldwork conversation? And what happens if we do not make a note of that potentially irrelevant observation? Worse still, what happens if we do not make a note and later find out that the observation would have been crucial and not irrelevant at all?

Once I started asking myself these questions, I quickly spiralled into a phase of worry, anxiety and self-doubt. I worried that my journal entries were not right, I was anxious about missing important work, and I seriously doubted my own judgement of knowing the important from the irrelevant, which obviously resulted in more worry and anxiety. With this chapter, I hope to alleviate some of these worries by specifically focusing on the developing a specific attitude towards journalling: the research journal should not be a chore or a cause for concern or worry. Of course, the research journal is a working document and part of the research journey, and the entries are particularly important during the fieldwork stage. But I am proposing that we should all approach our research journals with an attitude of openness, trust, playfulness, creativity and an expectation of fun.

The attitude I am advocating here is probably not quite what is expected in relation to research journals. However, this chapter merely continues the theme from Chapter 2 of myths around *the* research journal and what *the* research journal looks like. There are general assumptions of what a journal entry looks like: the form of long continuous prose recording deep reflections alongside highly insightful analyses. Therein lies the challenge. In everyday situations, we may not be able to provide such insightful analyses, or we may still be trying to make sense of our own reflections, or we may not feel like writing in long continuous prose. And so, the research journal has turned into something we must do, something that is onerous and tedious, when actually, the purpose of a research journal is to support the work we do during our research. A research journal should therefore not require additional labour and effort, even though it is a working document. Through approaching the research journal with that attitude of openness, trust, playfulness, creativity and the expectation of fun, we can learn to make the journal work for us. I am under no illusion, however. Even if we try to liberate ourselves from expectations and assumptions, we will still remain focused on 'getting it right' for our purposes.

Following on from here and building on the basic principles of journalling presented in Chapter 1, I offer prompts and ideas for what can be recorded in a research journal by drawing on different kinds of journalling that are commonly in use. I do so by specifically focusing on the aims, objectives and purposes of journalling, thereby balancing the academic and the scholarly with the personal, practical and pragmatic.

Note-taking as journalling

If one of the purposes of journalling is to keep a record of information to help us remember details, then note-taking needs to be seen as a form of journalling. Due to the assumptions and expectations we all have of *the* research journal, notes are often not seen as part of a research journal. How little we think of note-taking is exemplified in this quote from one of the contributors to this book when I asked for their permission to use some of their journal pages:

> I would be happy to share my notebook notes … it might be a stretch to call it a research journal.

In reality, however, note-taking plays an important role in the everyday life of a learner and researcher. Making notes is not only a process of putting on paper what we would like to commit to memory. In order to be able to take notes effectively, we need to comprehend what is in front of us, read between the lines and then decide what is relevant. Note-taking is a process of making sense and interpreting, analysing and contextualising, and in most cases, it is a process of multitasking, because we make sense, interpret, analyse and contextualise at the same time as we put those words onto paper that are to become our notes.

As reading and study notes probably make up a big proportion of entries in the research journal, it is worth spending some time organising these entries and considering where they will be recorded.

I have two kinds of reading and study notes: handwritten pages with a two-third/one-third split in a ring binder and computer-typed pages following the CaMLISd template. I find the handwritten pages useful for free-flowing notes, whereas the CaMLISd grid supports critical reading to develop a comprehensive literature review. CaMLISd is an acronym standing for Central argument (Ca), Methodology and methods (M), Limitations (L), Implications (I) and Similarities with and differences to other literature (Sd). (See https://policy. bristoluniversitypress.co.uk/making-the-most-of-your-research-journal/online-resources for guidance on how to use the CaMLISd grid and a link to download the template.) The basic principle is that the note-taking process is systematic. The advantages of the word template are that it focuses the reading and that once saved, notes can be added to, the more reading you undertake. The free-flow of the handwritten notes, by contrast, summarises the content without critique and critical commentary, therefore encouraging broader connections, which can be added into the one-third annotation column.

Another approach that should be mentioned here is visual note-taking, such as sketchnotes (Rohde, 2013) and mind maps (Buzan and Buzan, 2002, 2006). Both sketchnotes and mind maps are a particular form of note-taking that combine handwritten notes with visuals. The difference lies in their focus and emphasis. Where mind maps start from a central idea and develop outwards, sketchnotes have no particular layout or order to them. In this sense, the sketchnotes are more closely aligned with study notes or reading notes. Both forms are essentially a visual map or representation of contents. The advantage is that sketchnoting or mind mapping offer a different form of thinking and making sense as verbal contents are expressed in visual forms, especially when the contents are made up of abstract ideas and require conceptual developments (Fernández-Fontecha et al, 2019). As a consequence, the process of producing sketchnotes or mind maps is different to conventional note-taking and also requires practice (Erb, 2012). The end result is that the content remains more prominent in the mind because of the deep engagement and detailed sense-making that is required, and also that the notes are joyful to look at, and will therefore be looked at more often (Dimeo, 2016, 2017). In my own work I have experimented with sketchnotes that I have used as handouts (see Figure 3.1), and also with word clouds (see Figure 4.4).

For note-taking to be useful in the long term, it is important to keep detailed records of publications. In the moment of taking notes, it is all too easy to neglect detailed referencing or to forget noting the location where the file is saved on the computer. Similarly, during the note-taking process I recommend indicating if you have copied a phrase or sentence verbatim – make a note of the page number – or if you have paraphrased a section in your own words. Although these detailed notes may seem distracting or laborious at the time of note-taking, needing to track down a file or to identify a publication from its content or title only is by far more time-consuming, frustrating and often doomed to failure.

Figure 3.1: Nicole Brown's sketchnote to accompany a presentation about STEP

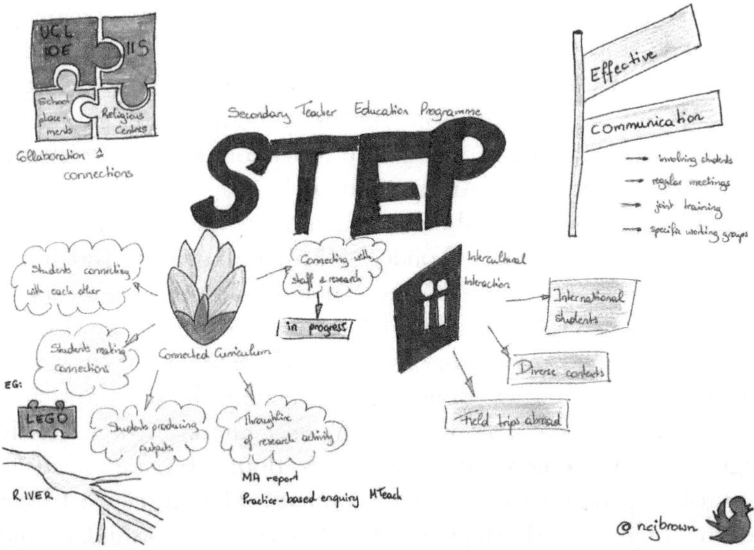

Lists and schedules as journal entries

Once we consider note-taking as a form of journalling, this opens up a whole host of contents that can be recorded in the research journal.

To-do lists

At its most elementary level, a research journal will consist of to-do lists. Carrying out research is not a linear process, and often comes with additional tasks, such as teaching and marking. Nowadays to-do lists can be maintained as part of diary and mailing programs and applications, which have the added benefit of supporting the management of the tasks through tagging, flagging, communicating, sharing and moving them. The most efficient to-do lists are those that consist of manageable tasks. Even if the task is to 'write the book', the to-do list should not actually say that, which may be an entry for the research pipeline or for target setting (see below). The tasks on the to-do list should be broken down into manageable chunks, such as 'write 500 words for the book' or 'write for 30 minutes'. In an ideal scenario, therefore, the research journal includes several to-do lists to cover short-term, daily tasks alongside medium-term activities and long-term goals.

The to-do list may also include tasks that are not immediately related to day-to-day duties or deadlines. For example, you may note publications that are relevant for your work and that you would like to acquire and read, or list names of people in your field whose work you would like to bear in mind and who you may want to contact for advice and feedback or simply to connect with. The 'people to follow up' list is particularly relevant after conferences or other networking events, where you will have collected the business cards of many delegates for a wide range of different reasons. A quick word of advice here – as you are given the business card, make a note on the back of the card where you have met that person and what you were talking about. This makes it much easier to make the entry in your research journal later and to compose follow-up emails that are both relevant and specific.

While to-do lists may not be considered a formal entry in a research journal, they are invaluable in helping us manage our time, making sure we are productive and effective, and thereby maintaining them contributes to our research journey in a broader sense.

To-do lists have two functions. First, they guide us in our planning, so we stay on track in our work. Second, they function as 'brain dumps' because having all of your tasks recorded in to-do lists means that you do not need to worry about forgetting any of them. As a result, you can focus on what is important: getting the tasks done.

Trackers

With the increased interest in the bullet journal, trackers have also become more important. In bullet journalling tracking is meant to support mindful reflections and to revaluate experiences as well as to focus on personal development for the future (Ayobi et al, 2018). In this sense, the tracking activities become a reflection of your life and your personality (Yiannouli, 2019). What is being tracked in the bullet journals include habits, moods, sleep patterns and symptoms as well as any combined version of these four elements (Ayobi et al, 2018), but may also relate to exercise, medication, films, recipes, books, music, household budgeting, travels and shopping. These categories can be detailed even further. For example, travel trackers may refer to travel planning, such as things you would like to see and do, or things that need to be organised and packed, to best travel moments, prompts for journalling on the travel or about the journey (Miller, 2017). The list is endless.

Although the full list of bullet journalling is a rather daunting affair, tracking particular kinds of activities and works in the context of a research journal is definitely beneficial. To-do lists and trackers are quite similar in their functions as they both serve as planning tools and brain dumps. In addition, however, trackers can be used as a record of achievements, as they are not related to immediate, short-term tasks, but longer term developments. What exactly is being tracked and what the precise format of such a tracker looks like are very personal choices, but the most commonly used trackers in the contexts of research and academic careers are those relating to targets, research expenses, project management, ideas and achievements.

Tracking targets

Targets come in many forms. You may have specific targets regarding the publication process, your research work or your career development more broadly. Target setting has a long tradition in education, and as with all target setting, the targets need to meet specific criteria for the process to be effective. While the target-setting process and its efficacy have been the focus of debate for several decades (see, for example, Thanssoulis, 1999; Gann, 2002; Hall, 2009; Day and Tosey, 2011), the general consensus remains that targets need to be SMART or CUTE (see, for example, Werle Lee, 2010), with research indicating that CUTE targets may be more effective than SMART targets (see, for example, Bridgewater, 2011). Since its original conception (Doran, 1981) the acronym SMART has been subject to some changes, but is nowadays largely understood to mean Specific, Measurable, Achievable, Relevant and Time-bound, with CUTE standing for Comprehensive, Understandable, Time-bound and Enabling. Irrespective of which of the acronyms or measures for good targets are used, the aim is the same: to provide guidance and to set the target-setter up for success.

The following image (see Figure 3.2), taken from Lesley Price's research journal, is a practical example of a target tracker. Lesley is a Senior Teaching Fellow and Programme Leader in the Academic Writing Centre at the UCL Institute of Education in the UK. Managing student experiences and facilitating student learning with the related administrative and practical tasks alongside developing and carrying out research requires a special level of efficacy.

Lesley simply records the tasks that need to be completed with a date when they need to be finished by, thereby prioritising the tasks. Once a task is fulfilled, she makes a note in her records. The process is simple, but very effective, as she is able to see the relevant information at a glance.

Figure 3.2: Lesley Price's target tracker

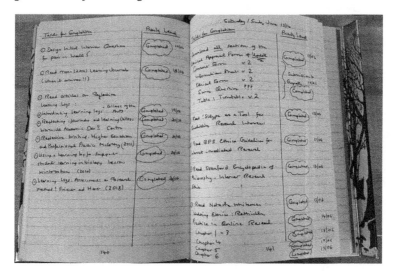

Finance tracker

In the messiness and rushes of everyday life, it is often the mundane tasks that are forgotten or overlooked. Within the context of research such mundane activities relate to administrative duties such as managing budgets and paperwork. Most universities have a specific system of how grant monies are allocated within the larger budgets and how research expenses may then be claimed back. In my own institution, there are budget codes against which any outgoings are costed. Within the finance department, the codes are generated systematically. To me, the budget codes are a meaningless combination of random numbers, which I forget the minute I receive them. Maintaining an effective finance tracker is therefore really helpful, not just to ensure that the budget is spent appropriately and wisely, but also to have one page to turn to, where all the relevant information is stored when it comes to claiming expenses with the relevant codes. The finance tracker can be a really simple spreadsheet that records the relevant budget codes, when money was spent on what, how much money of the allocated budget remains, whether or not the expenses were claimed back, and whether or not the expenses have been repaid. My own finance tracker is a handwritten page in one of my physical journals, as can be seen in Figure 3.3.

Figure 3.3: Nicole Brown's finance tracker

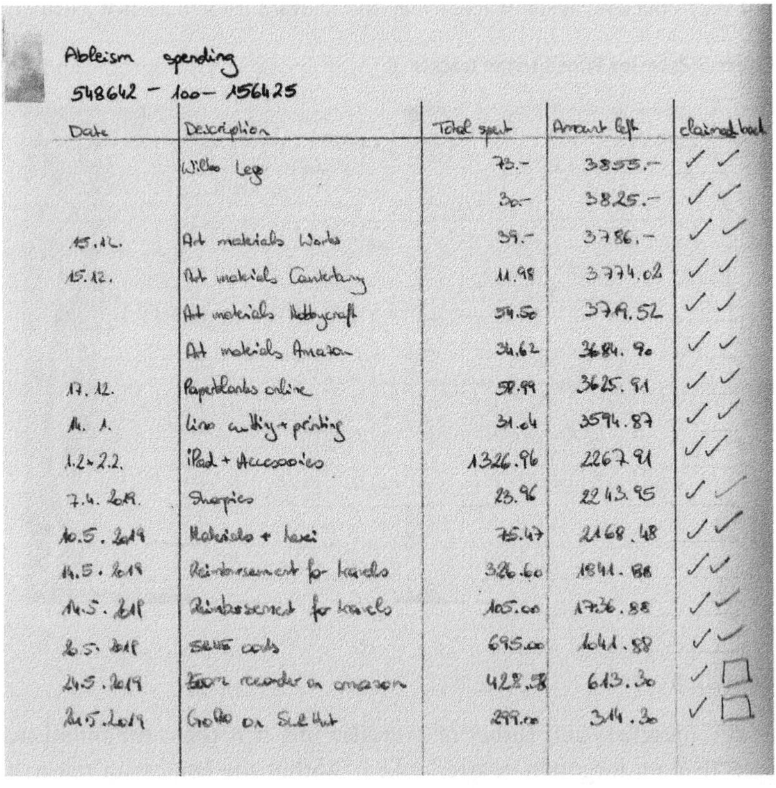
Ableism spending
548642 – 100 – 156425

Date	Description	Total spent	Amount left	claimed back
	Willow Leg	73.–	3855.–	✓ ✓
		30.–	3825.–	✓ ✓
15.12.	Art materials Works	39.–	3786.–	✓ ✓
15.12.	Art materials Canterbury	11.98	3774.02	✓ ✓
	Art materials Hobbycraft	54.50	3719.52	✓ ✓
	Art materials Amazon	34.62	3684.90	✓ ✓
17.12.	Paperblanks online	58.99	3625.91	✓ ✓
14.1.	lino cutting + printing	31.04	3594.87	✓ ✓
1.2.–2.2.	iPad + Accessories	1326.96	2267.91	✓ ✓
7.4.2019.	Sharpies	23.96	2243.95	✓ ✓
10.5.2019	Materials + [illegible]	75.47	2168.48	✓ ✓
14.5.2019	Reimbursement for travels	326.60	1841.88	✓ ✓
14.5.2019	Reimbursement for travels	105.00	1736.88	✓ ✓
16.5.2019	[illegible] cards	695.00	1041.88	✓ ✓
24.5.2019	Zoom recorder on amazon	428.58	613.30	✓ ☐
24.5.2019	GoPro on [illegible]	299.00	314.30	✓ ☐

What is not visible in this extract is that on the right-hand side of this double page there are notes of the grant conditions and how monies may be spent or were allocated in the funding proposals. There is usually some leeway for changes during research projects, but I find it helpful to identify where the main spending should go. (Go to https://policy.bristoluniversitypress.co.uk/making-the-most-of-your-research-journal/online-resources to download a template for an expenses tracker.)

Project management: the research pipeline

The research pipeline describes the process of publication from inception through to publication (Lebo, 2016). When you have one or maybe two projects to manage, project management is relatively simple. However, the more time you invest in collaborating with colleagues and developing broader networks, and the bigger the projects become, the more difficult it is to keep in mind the different tasks, goals and deadlines. To this end, keeping track of the various stages a project is in makes the entire process more manageable and helps tackle specific elements in a targeted way. An effective research pipeline tracker will take into account the different stages of the process while focusing on the end goal (Covey, 1989). How the research pipeline is tracked depends on personal preferences, but I have seen it done on whiteboards with post-it notes or as a page in research journals. The stages that need to be considered usually include: (1) idea and collaborators, (2) proposal, (3) literature review, (4) ethics, (5) data collection, (6) data analysis, (7) draft writing, (8) submission, (9) follow-up and (10) production and completion. (Go to https://policy.bristoluniversitypress.co.uk/making-the-most-of-your-research-journal/online-resources for guidance on how to use the research pipeline and a link to download a template.) The basic principle is to simply identify the projects you have on the go, prepare your spreadsheet, and tick the relevant boxes or put post-it notes into the relevant box on the grid.

The following image (see Figure 3.4) is an example of a completed research pipeline from Dr Lauren Ackerman, a Research Associate at Newcastle University in the UK.

As you can see, Lauren's approach to the research pipeline is quite similar to the one I have described, although she has merged some of my separate categories into the phases 'Data', 'Writing' and 'Submission'. Lauren also uses colours and patterns to signify the different stages of completion each project is in within each of the

Figure 3.4: Lauren Ackerman's research pipeline

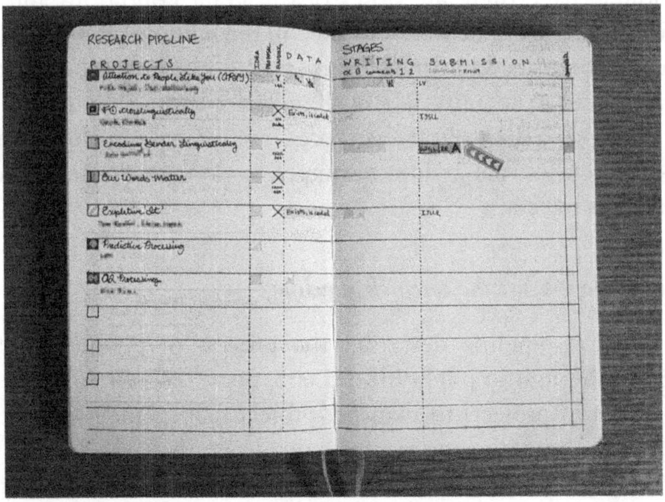

phases. As in Lauren's example, if you have several projects on the go, they will be at different stages, but ideally you will always have some articles in the process and some ideas in the pipeline.

Ideas tracker

As the research pipeline only tracks specific projects that are in the works and on the go, you may want to consider an ideas tracker in addition to the research pipeline. The ideas tracker is literally just a list of ideas you have for which you have not got any time or collaborators *now*, but which you would like to follow up *in the future*. Often, ideas come to us at times when we are at our busiest, when we cannot follow up on them. If we do not record those ideas, we lose them like fleeting thoughts, which we know were there, yet cannot quite grasp or hold on to. My ideas tracker is an old, plastic food box with study cards. Each card holds one idea because the space of the card enables me to add more thoughts to the initial idea to formulate a more coherent project from that. When I am at a loose end and stuck for ideas, I take out my ideas and evaluate them for their viability. Some ideas go back in the box; others stay out and become the focus of a new project. As with the to-do lists and other trackers, the ideas box functions as a 'brain dump' at busy times, but it also works as a starting point for times when creativity is not so easy to come by.

Recording achievements

From maintaining to-do lists and trackers like the research pipeline and the ideas box the step towards tracking targets and achievements is quite natural. Indeed, the lists and trackers themselves are evidence and records of achievements, as they are completed. However, demonstrating skills and knowledge is more complex in academia, as skills, knowledge and achievement need to be evidenced when applying for a lectureship, for promotion, for research or teaching fellowships, for professional development qualifications and for grants. In each of these circumstances the achievements and development required differ, as the emphasis of the roles and responsibilities varies. In such situations, the research journal can provide a professional narrative and overview.

Even if individuals do not associate the records of achievements as entries in a research journal, many academics do maintain a 'full' CV. The principle of a full CV is merely to keep a record of all the activities related to professional and developmental work in higher education. Whenever any evidence is required for applications, a relevant letter, expression of interest or CV can be developed by selecting the applicable sections, activities and achievements from the full CV. (Go to https://policy.bristoluniversitypress.co.uk/ making-the-most-of-your-research-journal/online-resources to download a template for a full CV.)

Journalling from the field

Journal entries emerging from journalling in the field are probably the closest to what we would expect journal entries to look like. These are the kinds of entries we expect to be written in long prose form providing detailed insight into our innermost reflections and deepest thoughts, the basic principles of diary-keeping. This expectation is further compounded due to the prevailing discourses and debates of reflexivity across all disciplines, from anthropology to science studies (Alvesson and Skoldberg, 2000; Etherington, 2004). Although scholars and philosophers have practised reflexivity in some form since the Ancient Greeks (Lawson, 1985), it was during the 20th century that the simultaneous occurrence of an increased interest and loss of confidence in self, identity and way of knowing led to a reflexive turn in research (Foley, 2002). What has arisen from this crisis in confidence, trust and knowledge is the understanding that researchers:

> still speak as mere mortals from various historical, culture-bound standpoints ... [and] ... still make limited, historically situated knowledge claims. (Foley, 2002: 487)

Thus, the reflexive turn in research has enabled us to see researchers as who they are within the research process, instead of seeing them as all-knowing and objective, distanced from their work. In every research, the researcher is present and the researcher's world view shapes questions and experiments. There is now a wealth of literature highlighting how within analytical processes the researcher shapes the themes and develops theorisations, even if research reports often present themes as 'emergent' or 'emerging' (see, for example, Chiseri-Strater, 1996; Braun and Clarke, 2006, 2019; MacLure, 2011; James, 2013; Chadwick, 2017; Morgan, 2018; Humble and Radina, 2019; Ellingson and Sotirin, 2020). Yet, journalling about reflexivity and self-introspection is only a small part of what journalling from the field is, can and should be.

Synthesising the guidance provided in research handbooks and publications on writing fieldnotes, there are three groups of content that should be considered in research journals: observations and conversations, emotions and experiences, and thoughts and reflections. Categories and typologies are notoriously complex because of their arbitrary nature, which is no different here. Thoughts and reflections, for example, may equally count as emotions and experiences; observations and conversations may also be linked to or tied up with thoughts and reflections, and indeed, emotions and experiences. However, the categorisation into these three areas is useful when considering the level of interpretation and analysis used within those categories.

The first level of recording relates to observations and conversations as a descriptive, factual account of what is happening. Within the context of research, therefore, observations and conversations are most commonly recorded in the course of data collection. Whether as researchers we carry out an ethnography in the field, experiments in a laboratory or interviews with participants, the details we see and hear constitute the backbone of our data collection, and therefore a significant amount of data. Depending on disciplines and research designs, the descriptive accounts may relate to observations of people and their behaviours, but may also, of course, relate to the differences as variables are observed in laboratory experiments. However, it should be mentioned here that observations and conversations that are not intrinsically linked with the data collection phase of the research may still be relevant and noteworthy. Such observations or conversations may happen as part of conferences and networking events, or, in relation to supervision, mentoring and staff development meetings.

Emotions and experiences represent a second level of detailing because we are making sense of what is going on. In some ways, emotions and experiences link in with the first level of recording because we notice and observe our emotions and experiences in response to what we have heard or seen. Yet, in order to be able to record emotions and experiences, we need to interpret, analyse and reflect in ways that go beyond the immediate factual, descriptive recording of observations. In the course of the everyday, this initial, provisionary analysis tends to happen subconsciously, so that on a personal, subjective level there is only a very fine line between an observation and an observed emotion.

Thoughts and reflections describe the third level of interpretation and analysis, a meta-level of reflecting on and thinking about what was recorded in the observations and conversations or what was identified in the context of emotions and experiences. Whereas the analytical, sense-making process occurs so quickly that it is sometimes barely noticeable, the interpretation and analysis at this third level occurs as a conscious, purposeful and intentional activity. At this level of recording, we will develop interpretations that may be recorded as separate analyses or simply as annotations to the previously recorded observations or emotions.

While it does not matter for us journallers to categorise our entries and keep emotions and thoughts separate from conversations, for example, it is important to remember the three different levels of analysis to ensure variety of entries. When writing a journal entry, it may well be that you only attend to the descriptive elements of observations, initially, to make sure you have that record. Later, when there is more time, you may want to consider your emotions and experiences in that moment or reflect on what you have observed, and add to that. As Chapter 4 outlines how to record and Chapter 5 details the considerations of when to record, suffice to say here that not everything needs to be done at once or all the time and only in writing. Yet, during the course of a research journey, journalling should not remain on the superficial, descriptive level for all entries, as critical thought and reflection are key to originality and significant contributions in research.

Practical journalling concerns

At the end of this chapter, I would like to return to two particular concerns arising from the content presented here: the practicalities of maintaining a journal and getting the entries right.

Once you have decided what you will record in your journal you may want to return to Chapter 2 to consider different formats, shapes, paper and writing implements. You may want to journal some elements of your work electronically, with others in a journal. One interesting example for a research journal comes from Associate Professor Raul Pacheco-Vega, a political scientist and geographer, whose interdisciplinary research lies at the intersection of space, public policy, environment and society. Raul uses what he calls an 'Everything Notebook' to record everything: to-do lists, article summaries, thinking through ideas, notes to himself and the like. Figures 3.5 and 3.6 are examples of two pages from his Everything Notebook. Figure 3.5 shows a page of notes Raul took when Dr Peter Matthews guest lectured on homelessness policy in a Public Policy

Figure 3.5: Raul Pacheco-Vega's lecture notes

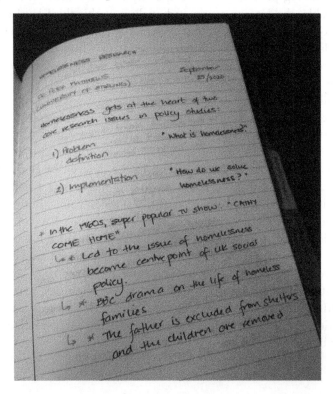

Analysis course. Figure 3.6 shows Raul's weekly to-do list broken down by day. Most times, Raul tries to work on three things per day.

Figure 3.6: Raul Pacheco-Vega's to-do list

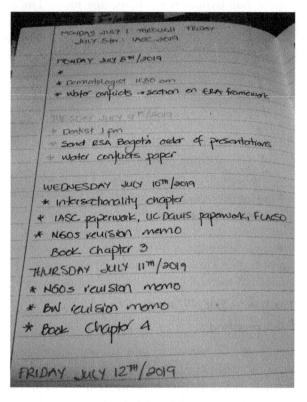

As is evident from the photographs, Raul has developed a system of tabbing and referencing along with different coloured pens to help him navigate his Everything Notebook. How exactly he manages and organises his journal is described in detail on his website (www. raulpacheco.org/resources/the–everything–notebook). Yet, it should be repeated here that ultimately every person needs to find their own best way of journalling.

Let me now also return to what was said in the chapter introduction about getting the entries right and about knowing or deciding what is relevant and what is not. In short, recording and writing entries in a research journal are choices that we make as researchers. This may mean we potentially overlook important information at a specific point in time because it appears irrelevant, but turns out not to be irrelevant later on.

However, this does not mean that we need to record everything all the time. Instead, we should be confident to trust our own gut feelings, even if they do sometimes prove us wrong. The choices we are making as researchers relating to entries in a research journal are not dissimilar to holidaymakers on sightseeing tours. The person on vacation can consistently take dozens of photographs of the landmarks they see, literally from every angle and perspective; or they can decide to take one snapshot and enjoy the atmosphere, the sounds, the smells. The busy photographer may well have solid records of 'what was seen', but may not be able to recount 'what it felt like' to have been where they were. This is the same predicament we experience as researchers. If we were to constantly make notes and entries, we would develop a very narrow field of vision, almost tunnel-like, focusing on specific aspects of what is happening, instead of being able to make wider connections and seeing the bigger picture. This is where the open, confident, trusting attitude is key. Rather than worrying too much about all the details and thereby losing track, it is important to 'live' the research process consciously and intentionally.

Living the research process consciously and intentionally in this way may mean that certain choices that are made are not ideal, that some details are missed or that there are simply not enough entries or notes. Let me say this: by being a little more relaxed about my own recording habits and not feeling pressured to 'get it right' I have overcome my worries and anxieties to such an extent that my journalling has become regular and consistent, leading to more meaningful entries. In addition, as shown in Chapter 4, there are templates and strategies to systematically develop entries from memory. Thus, there are opportunities to catch up with what has been missed, and so there really is no need to worry.

TRY THIS!

Take note(s)

You can embed this exercise in your everyday working pattern. The next time you need to read a journal article, try out the three different ways for taking reading notes presented in this chapter: a CaMLISd grid, handwritten notes and sketchnotes or mind maps. Once you have tried out all three approaches, consider what you have gained or lost through each.

Train your senses

You can do this exercise anywhere, at home, in a garden or park, in a cafe or at university, and you can do this as many times as you would like to in different environments. You can also do this as one 50-minute exercise working through one sense immediately after another (sight, sound, smell, taste and touch) or as five exercises of 10 minutes only:

Take time for 4 minutes to become aware of your surroundings. Set yourself a timer for that. After 4 minutes, set your timer to 2 minutes and focus on one sense only. Immerse yourself totally in what you hear or what you see or feel. Do not use focus on more than one sense at this stage. After 1 minute has lapsed, record what you have focused on and noticed (for example, seen or heard or felt) in whichever way feels comfortable. You may, for example, write what you have seen, or talk into your voice recorder or create a drawing. It does not matter how you record, but you should try to record as much as possible of what you have seen or heard or felt. Do this for 4 minutes. Then you can either end the activity or do the exercise again, using a different sense. Reflect on what you have noticed and learned from the exercise and what you can glean from what you have recorded.

Check out journalling ideas

The internet is truly awash with ideas for journalling. Of course, the nature of the internet is that websites appear and disappear depending on trends. It is therefore difficult to recommend specific links. Instead, I am recommending specific search terms and hashtags, so that you may be able to find inspiration and ideas for what to record and how to design the layout of the individual pages so that the recording becomes enjoyable:

– On Pinterest and Instagram, the hashtags to follow are, for example, 'bulletjournal', 'bujo', 'artjournalling' (or 'artjournaling'), 'journalling' (or 'journaling'), 'moodtrackers', 'habittrackers', 'bujoinspiration', 'bujoemotions', 'planner' and 'bujoideas'.
– Terms or phrases to enter into search engines include, for example, 'bullet journal ideas', 'creative bullet journal ideas', 'bullet journal inspiration' and 'essential bullet journal ideas'.
– More specifically, you may want to search ideas for 'daily spreads', 'weekly layouts', 'monthly spreads', 'budget tracker', 'habit tracker', 'goal tracker' or 'bullet journal tracker ideas'.

Go to https://policy.bristoluniversitypress.co.uk/making-the-most-of-your-research-journal/online-resources for:

• Guidance on how to use the CaMLISd grid and a template
• A template for an expenses tracker
• Guidance on how to use the research pipeline and a template
• A template for a full CV
• The figures in full-sized format and colour

4

How to record in a research journal?

Chapter aims

- To offer strategies and tools for research journalling beyond pen and paper.

- To highlight the processes of research journalling, such as within fictionalisation.

- To consider technological tools to support research journalling.

Introduction

Chapter 3 has shown that what constitutes an entry to a research journal may vary from to-do lists and trackers through to notes from the field. What has yet to be discussed, however, is what the notes from the field may look like. As has been stated, the aim of this book is to provide practical guidance for making the most of a research journal, but also to demonstrate the scope and opportunities of journalling. If we have misconceptions about what a research journal looks like and what we should record, then these misconceptions also seep into the question of how entries should be recorded.

Guidance around ethnographic fieldnotes reconfirms the myth that there is a particular pattern of working and way of recording: getting notes down in the field to formulate detailed descriptions at the end of the day (Emerson et al, 2011) and memoing or memo writing, as in the way it is associated with Grounded Theory (Charmaz, 2006). Although qualitative researchers regularly apply these ways of working, scholars have noted methodological and practical concerns: first, disciplinary conventions and trends dictate the kind of note-taking or recording that happens (Rapport, 1991). Second, note-taking and recording fieldnotes are processes that often reproduce existing knowledge and skills because records are written from the positionality of the researcher's own background, tacit knowledge and implicit beliefs

(Wolfinger, 2002). And third, even well-known ethnographers are not able to fully articulate what happens or what exactly it is they do when they decide what to record (Walford, 2009). This not-knowing-what-happens during the recording process is itself reflected in the messiness of the fieldnotes and the entries in the research journal, which are used as a basis to make sense (Malinowski, 1961; Clifford, 1990).

As a response to these critiques, interest in the processes of writing fieldnotes and recording journal entries has increased with publications specifically focusing on providing guidance for effective notes (Phillippi and Lauderdale, 2018), on using fieldnotes as datasets in themselves (Pacheco-Vega, 2019) or on supporting critical reflection (Maharaj, 2016). The increased relevance placed on fieldnotes and researchers' recognition of the limitations of what is recorded and how (Walford, 2009) has resulted in the development of creative, playful forms of recording (Nolas and Varvantakis, 2019). Turns in the social sciences towards reflexive, narrative and creative arts-based approaches (Foley, 2002; Kara, 2020; Leavy, 2020b), and the heightened awareness of writing as a method of inquiry (Richardson, 2000, 2003; Prendergast, 2009; Faulkner, 2017; Phillips and Kara, 2021), have further resulted in the understanding that the 'how' of ways of working is not uniform, and so could and should be open to change.

Bearing in mind these preliminary thoughts, this chapter highlights that research journals do not necessarily have to follow any specific rules, and do not even have to be in written formats. Instead, I provide an insight into pragmatic note-taking and software-assisted record-keeping alongside creative approaches to reflections and recording, such as photography and videos, soundscapes and music, as well as more analytical representations, installations and collages. After all, what is recorded can be descriptive, factual accounts, but also syntheses and analyses.

Templates as journal entries

Drawing on the ideas of effective journalling through maintaining a bullet journal, recording entries for the research does not necessarily mean writing long passages in prose. Sometimes, recording may be more meaningful with recording sheets, observation and coding templates. As always, we have to remind ourselves of the marathon runner in the wetsuit: the method needs to fit the purpose. In the tradition of ethnographic fieldnotes, observations can be recorded as notes, which are then formulated into continuous prose with detailed, thick descriptions. However, targeted observations may also be recorded through templates developed for the particular purpose of noting down relevant behaviours, for example. This form of note-taking is quite commonly used in survey designs or experiments within positivist research frameworks. Indeed, coding and tallying do lend themselves to a more quantitative data collection approach. Yet, if the observation sheet is set up purposefully, it is possible to record qualitative observations quickly and efficiently. One such productive example for an observation

Figure 4.1: London School of Hygiene and Tropical Medicine's observation template

---

Appendix N Example structured observation tool

Complete only after gaining informed consent of drug seller and client.

Client ID |___|___|___|___|___|___|___| Researcher Initials |___|___|___|

Drug seller (DS)ID |___|___|___| AUDIO No. |_____| ; |_____|

Date |___|___/___|___/___|___| Start time ____:____ End time____:_____

1. a. Record the initial interaction between the drug seller and client:

_____

_____

_____

_____

   b. Is client seeking medication for themselves □ or someone else □ (who_____)?

   c. Does client ask for a specific drug □ or consult the drug seller □?

   d. Does DS ask what drug the client wants □ or does DS enter a consultation with the client □?

2. a. Does DS ask if client already sought medical help elsewhere? □ Yes □ No

   b. Did client attend elsewhere before here? □ Yes □ No

   c. If Yes, where? □ Another drug seller (order_____name_____)

      (and order)   □ A private health facility (order_____name_____)

                     □ A public health facility (order_____name_____)

                     □ Other (order_____name_____)

   d. If Yes, does the client give an explanation for why they attended elsewhere first? □ Yes □ No

      Detail _____

      _____

      _____

4. a. Does DS ask about patient symptoms? □ Yes □ No

   b. What symptoms does the client report?

      Fever □   Cough □   Vomit □   Diarrhoea □   Difficulty breathing □   Abdominal pain □   Headache □

   c. Client reported age and sex of patient: (years/ months/wks) |___|___|___| / |___|___| / |___|___|
      □ Male □ Female

OR d. Researcher estimate of patient age and sex: □<12 months □< 5 years □< 15 years □>15 years
      □ Male □ Female

---

template (see Figure 4.1) comes from the London School of Hygiene and Tropical Medicine consortium guidance relating to the study of the behaviours of pharmacists (drug seller, DS) and their customers (client) (no 3 not in the original) (Chandler and Reynolds, 2013: 58).

While there are still sections that need to be completed in free writing, there are many qualitative details that can be gleaned from merely ticking a box, such as who the customer is buying the medication for (Question 1b) or which symptoms the customer reports (Question 4b). The advantage of such a detailed recording template is that observations are systematic and focused, and may even be outsourced to others without losing that structure. The drawbacks of such detailed templates are that they need to be designed carefully in advance, often with some insight into what to expect of the observations, and that other elements of the observation are lost or neglected because there is literally no space or scope to put additional notes. This brings us back to the question of purpose and aim. If the aim is to observe and record behaviours, then a detailed template is probably more motivating for the journaller than the thought of needing to capture all of the information in free writing. If the aim is to add a layer of interpretation, to therefore link into the analytical stages of emotions and experiences or thoughts and reflections or to make notes of conversations as they happen, then a template like the one presented above is probably more distracting than helpful.

Journalling with models of reflection

What needs to be considered is that templates are available in a variety of designs or layouts and may follow different principles. The models of reflective practice presented in Chapter 1 are, in effect, also templates to structure and systematise thought processes and function as sense-making strategies. Models of reflective practice may therefore be particularly useful templates in connection with the analytical stages of emotions and experiences or thoughts and reflections. It is notoriously difficult to teach reflective practice (Rogers, 2001; Mena-Marcos et al, 2013; Toom et al, 2015) because as journallers we must learn to avoid superficiality (Fook et al, 2006), and instead engage systematically with our experiences by drawing on theories.

As the aim of reflective models is to help improve professional practices, not all models are equally suited for research purposes. The most naturally applicable models of reflection for research journalling are probably the models by Graham Gibbs (1988) and Stephen Brookfield (1995). In brief, the reflective model, according to Gibbs

(1988), is cyclical in nature, leading from observations and sense-making to drawing conclusions, which form the basis of a personal action plan. Brookfield's (1995) model of reflection suggests employing four lenses, thus four different perspectives from which to view the same event. After the initial autobiographical perspective, journallers are asked to reflect on the same circumstances and situations by putting themselves into the shoes of colleagues and students. By taking this particular stance it is possible to distance ourselves somewhat from the personal experiences and to view the given situations more analytically and empathetically. The fourth perspective relates to the theoretical lens, which requires us to engage with literature to make sense of experiences and gain relevant insights and explanations for the future. Although an emphasis on professional development is implicit in these models of reflection, these two reflective models can also be easily adapted to suit the purpose of research journalling. In the case of the model by Gibbs (1988), you may want to skip the evaluation stage of the model, but then reengage with the analysis and conclusion. Similarly, for Brookfield's (1995) model, you may want to reconsider whose shoes you are trying to step into. Instead of the students' views, you may want to analyse the views of research participants or stakeholders before you reengage with the model and its theoretical lens.

However, it should be said that academics do teach, and so part of the research journal may become related to teaching practice. For the sake of completeness, therefore, I refer you to the online resources for a description of five different models of reflection (see https:// policy.bristoluniversitypress.co.uk/making-the-most-of-your-research-journal/online-resources).

Fictionalisation and poetic inquiry

If journalling with models of reflection is considered as drawing on an eclectic mix of data sources, such as memories and literature, to make sense of an experience, then the step from recording through those templates to fictionalisations and poetic inquiries is not quite so daunting. The process of completing a template for reflective practice is making sense in writing, and the production of fiction or poetry also draws on writing as a method of inquiry (Richardson, 2000; 2003). The advantage of using fiction or poetry for research journalling is that this form of writing is not merely recording facts or descriptions, but opens up analytical and interpretative opportunities. The process of writing and analysing through fiction and poetry is a creative approach to illuminating data and to extrapolating meaning that would otherwise stay hidden or forgotten (Ellingson, 2009, 2017). Developing and employing a variety of texts allows researchers to tend to different kinds of truths and experiences:

> not to evoke a sense of empathy, cultural insight or deep significance, but to confront us with the *radical specificity* of living a life ... in the sense that life is lived in the flows, multiplicities, and provisionality of each moment, event, emotion. (Sotirin, 2010, section 6; original emphasis)

Writers of fictionalised accounts and poetry, as are common in narrative research, evocative (auto)ethnography, creative nonfiction and other forms of artistic research practices, rely on structure, characterisation and literary tools in their work (Leavy, 2016). This artistic fictionalisation allows for research to become transformational, expressive and evocative (Barone and Eisner, 2012; Leavy, 2020b).

The following image (Figure 4.2) is an example from the research journal of Aine McAllister, a lecturer at UCL Institute of Education and poet from the Glens of Antrim in Northern Ireland. Aine's research interest lies in ethnopoetics, a particular form of narrative

Figure 4.2: Aine McAllister's poetic inquiry

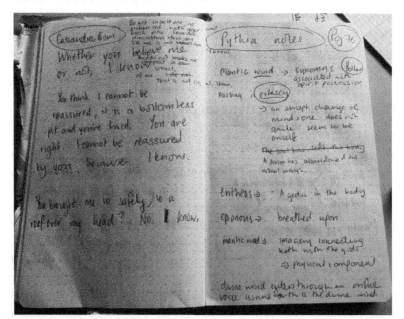

analysis, inquiry and methodology at the intersection of anthropology, linguistics, comparative literature and folklore, to analyse and understand voice (Blommaert, 2006). As such, Aine's way of working is probably more naturally inclined towards poetry. Yet, as journallers we should look at her process to gain an insight into the creative mechanisms and to be inspired for our own writing of poetry or fiction.

What stands out in this example is Aine's engagement with the entry for the research journal. The notes made on the right-hand page refer to an article that challenges the notion that the words the Pythia spoke during divine consultations were reformulated afterwards by priests for them to make sense (Maurizio, 1995). Aine engaged with comparative anthropological and historical literature to fictionalise a character based on the Pythia through which she would explore the theme of voice. Aine is not merely recording, but actively making sense, interpreting, analysing and manipulating perspectives, which leads to the development of poetic ideas and fictionalised, experiential moments.

Employing such an arts-based analytical process does not mean that data can be moulded along figments of imaginations. Instead, the journaller's responsibility is to draw out and represent the complexity of data. Evocativeness, expressiveness and transformation are not intentional but natural by-products of drawing on literary devices and the emotional connectivity that is reinforced in these forms of writing. The main consideration when writing fiction and poetry relates again to the purpose. There is a difference in how you may approach the writing process if you are merely trying to make sense of experiences to if you intend to share the end product publicly as part of your research dissemination.

Producing fiction or poetry as a form of inquiry requires skill, knowledge and practice (Prendergast et al, 2009; Leavy, 2016; Faulkner, 2019). Unfortunately, for many of us fiction writing and the creation of poetry are inextricably linked with our educational experiences in literature lessons, and often associated with enormous amounts of effort and concentration, as well as embarrassment and humiliation. As a consequence, we shy away from exploring the opportunities these forms of writing may bring. In his book *The Ode Less Travelled: Unlocking the Poet Within*, Stephen Fry aims to demystify the process of composing poetry by providing ideas for how to structure poems, but also by emphasising the pleasure and enjoyment that may be gained from the process. Ultimately, the research journal is your opportunity to engage in all forms of writing and to be playful in your approach to recording thoughts, reflections and analyses.

Playing with words

If fictionalisations and poetic inquiries require skill, knowledge and practice and are associated with feelings of dread and worry, then perhaps being creative and playful when recording observations and conversations, emotions and experiences and thoughts and reflections is a first step towards gaining confidence. At the same time, using phrases or words as a form of expression may in itself open up new insights and understandings. The emphasis here is again on recording what feels noteworthy and what resonates.

Figure 4.3: Nicole Brown's compete, compete, complete

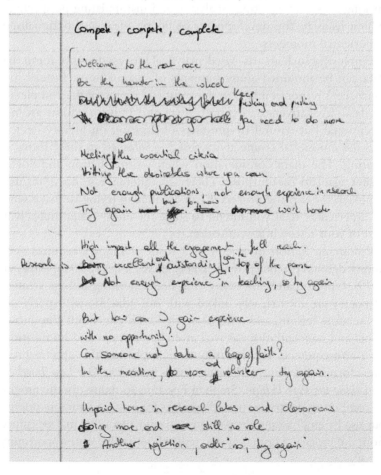

The following two images (see Figures 4.3 and 4.4) are entries from my own research journals that exemplify the idea of playing with words.

In this first example, I was trying to process my own thoughts and feelings, but also those of colleagues, at a time when we all felt frustrated with our experiences at work. Although we all had different educational experiences, we struggled with reconciling the collaborative nature of teaching and learning from previous careers with the competitiveness in academia. The format or shape of my writing may appear poem-like, which was not intentional, as I only followed the natural flow of my thoughts. Where I paused to think, I started a new 'paragraph' or 'stanza'. By playing with phrases as they popped into my head, I was able to record my observations and synthesise conversations while also giving voice to the frustration felt by all of us. As such, the journal entry provides a snapshot of the experiences of early career researchers in the neoliberal academy.

The second example is also a playful experiment with words to capture particular emotions and experiences, but looks quite different.

Figure 4.4: Nicole Brown's word cloud

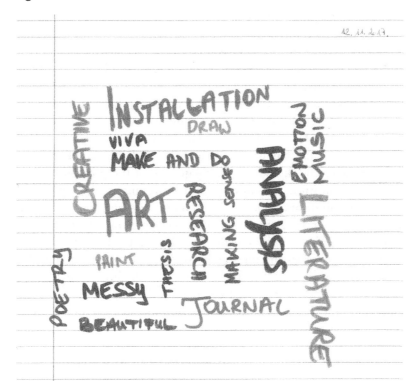

For the playing with words presented in Figure 4.4, I used different coloured pens to manually generate a word cloud to record what captured my imagination and affected me at the time. I was working on my doctoral research and was trying to make sense of that journey, but found that I was becoming increasingly drawn into areas of analyses and communication that drifted away from the compilation of a thesis to be defended in a viva.

I understand that this word cloud will not be particularly meaningful to anyone other than myself, but that was the whole purpose of this form of recording. Playing with words enabled me to reflect on my hopes and worries and to commit them to paper, and there was never any intention of sharing that particular word cloud or of using it in future work. It felt enjoyable and cathartic. On other occasions, I manually created word clouds to synthesise my impressions from readings, lectures or conversations – and I still do, actually. For me, playing with words in this way takes the pressure off conventional journalling with the end result that I journal more regularly.

Making and doing as journal entries

Writing or playing with words are not the only ways to record observations and conversations, emotions and experiences, thoughts and reflections. Instead, we should look to further forms of communication and expression by building on Embodied Inquiry, an approach that centres on the body, embodiment and bodily experiences in research (Leigh and Brown, 2021). Embodied Inquiry is underpinned, among others, by three cornerstones to human understanding: (1) human understanding is intrinsically embodied (Finlay, 2015); (2) language is inaccurate and inefficient (Scarry, 1985; Sontag, 2003); and, as a consequence of the previous tenets, (3) communication and human understanding are metaphorical (Lakoff and Johnson, 2003). As communication and understanding are embodied and metaphorical, and language is not able to capture that level of embodied and metaphorical being, it follows that human communication goes and must go beyond verbal expression. In order to account for and address the beyond-verbal, Embodied Inquiry suggests drawing on arts-based research, as the arts are able to offer embodied and bodily connections that other approaches cannot. Specifically, arts-based research allows:

> to provide new insights and learning; to describe, explore, discover, problem-solve; to forge micro–macro connections;

to engage holistically; to be evocative and provocative; to raise awareness and empathy; to unsettle stereotypes, challenge dominant ideologies, and include marginalized voices and perspectives; and to open up avenues for public scholarship, usefulness and social justice. (Leavy, 2015: 21–7)

Bearing in mind these theoretical foundations along with the many functionalities and opportunities of the arts and arts-based research, an 'entry' in the research journal may therefore look radically different from writing or note-taking. The concept of art journalling was briefly introduced in Chapter 1 as a visual diary to record what happens in the moment, as a form of commentary or memory-making and memory-keeping. I have seen handcrafted examples, where individuals use knitting and crochet to track the temperature and sky formations throughout a year, or their personal moods at a particular period. Basically, the crafter creates a legend assigning a particular meaning to a colour, and then knits or crochets a pattern they have decided on. For example, dark blue yarn represents temperatures between −10°C and −5°C, or a feeling of stability, whereas lighter blue is for temperatures between −5°C and 0°C, or feeling balanced. Red may indicate temperatures above 30°C, and emotions associated with anger or love. Some crafters knit or crochet squares for each day or week, which are then sewn together as blankets; others knit or crochet two rows for each day or week to turn into a scarf. The outcomes are then temperature scarves or mood blankets. Figure 4.5 is one such example from Dr Madeline White, a researcher at Royal Holloway University in London. Madeline's expertise lies in the role of oral testimonies and historiographies within Holocaust Studies.

Within her research work Madeline is particularly interested in testimony as a narrative genre and the specificities of context of time, place and motivation embedded in such sources, and her scarves are no different. For Madeline, making temperature or sky scarves is an opportunity to feel present in the moment and pay attention to that moment, which may otherwise slip by without her noticing. When she knits that moment into a scarf, it then sits alongside 364 other moments that together tell the story of a year in Madeline's life. The scarves are therefore a method of journalling and memory-keeping, as well as works of art.

At this point, I would like to suggest using artists as an inspiration and to gain an insight into how they have recorded and commented on experiences. For example, Faith Ringgold, an American artist from Harlem, New York, best known for her paintings and textile

Figure 4.5: Madeline White's temperature scarf

arts, springs to mind. Her American People Series is a collection of paintings depicting racial tensions and the political landscape of the Civil Rights Movement in the United States of the 1960s. One of the most powerful paintings from that series is *American People Series #20: Die*, which can be viewed virtually from the Museum of Modern Art in New York. In a bid to distance herself from the Euro-Western traditions of paintings, she also used quilts to capture and express her experiences, identity and heritage as a Black woman. Quilting itself is a deeply embedded in African-American tradition, as slaves would often use symbols within their quilts to convey biblical and informational meanings. Ringgold's *The French Collection* series is particularly noteworthy.

Other interesting artists to consider are Joseph Cornell and Hannah Höch, for example. Hannah Höch was a German artist and a revolutionary within the arts world in many ways. As one of very few women artists in the early 20th century, she strongly and consciously advocated for women to work as creatives in society. She also developed new art techniques, and is nowadays considered the originator of photomontage. In one of her most widely known pieces, *The Beautiful Girl (Das schöne Mädchen)*, she used photomontage, a form of collaging with clippings from popular texts and magazines, to comment on the gender differences and power differentials between men and women in Weimar Germany. Joseph Cornell was an American artist who became most celebrated for his assemblages. He used boxes with glass panes, in which he arranged and exhibited collected items and photographs. His assemblage work is considered as deeply personal and mysterious, as it covers a wide range of themes, as reflected in the title of his boxes series such as the *Soap Bubble Sets*, the *Space Object Boxes* or the *Aviary* series.

I am not suggesting that we all aim to be the next Faith Ringgold, Joseph Cornell or Hannah Höch. I am merely recommending we look elsewhere for guidance and inspiration for creating journal entries, as ultimately, anything and everything goes. For some journallers among us, drawing, painting, sketching, collage-making and assemblage may come naturally to maintain a visual diary; for others, it may be sewing or quilting; others enjoy building LEGO® models; others, still, may feel more creative when they are cooking or baking. In Chapter 6, I outline what you can 'do' with entries that have been created through an arts-based approach, but for now, let us remind ourselves: anything and everything goes.

Technology for journalling

Many of the examples presented in this chapter so far have shown pen-and-paper-type recording for a research journal. In reality, many forms of journalling draw on or are supported by technology. The template for the models of reflection, for example, lends itself to be used with word processing software, which would allow for systematic tagging and saving as a digital file. Chapter 2 also introduced the possibility of multimedia journalling and blogs, vlogs and social media accounts as potential research journals. Depending on what is being recorded, technology may be quite a natural answer to how entries in a research journal can be made. For example, recording information at the level of observations and conversations is easily possible through simply saving blog posts, commentaries, social media posts or chat texts from WhatsApp or other messaging applications. Of course, ethical ground rules and ethical considerations apply (see Chapter 7), but in principle, 'how to record' does not need to be more complex than cutting and pasting. As has been said, the important factor in 'how to record' is the question of purpose and aim of the recording and the entry in the research journal. In my own work, I usually record conversations as part of data collection through interviews to facilitate transcription, for example. Yet, the sections where I comment or respond to what my research participants say, are in themselves relevant data that I use for further analyses later on. Chapter 6 offers more details about what to do with the entries, so suffice it to say here that recording my own thoughts, my voice, are helpful tools in the research process.

A great variety of digital recording devices are available on the market, and so it has taken me a long time to figure out which tools and gadgets would be most suitable for my purposes. My choices are obviously not necessarily the best choices for you, and yet, some guidance is always useful. In the following, I therefore offer basic examples of recording tools and gadgets with some advice on what to consider before you splash out on expensive gear.

Smartphone and/or tablet

The cheapest option for video and audio recording is to use a smartphone and/or tablet. Many of us own our personal gadgets, but there are also opportunities within universities and research institutes to borrow smartphones and/or tablets cheaply or completely free of charge. In addition to the cost considerations, the biggest advantage of using smartphones and/or tablets is that you will have your gadgets on you. Smartphones are more practical in many ways than tablets, simply for their size – they are easier to hold for recordings than tablets. If you are a regular tablet user, you may just want to invest in a cheap stand or cover that turns into a stand, so that you can record without having to hold the tablet for a long period of time. The quality of photographs and videos of smartphones and tablets is quite astonishing, and in most instances, even the audio recordings are clear, although background noises do impact the quality of the audio tracks. As such, smartphones and/or tablets are a really valid and viable option. However, one concern with smartphones and/or tablets relates to data management. Before you start recording hour-long tracks, make sure that you have enough storage and that you know how you will be able to transfer the data from your gadget to your main computer or university hard drive. Knowing about data storage and transfer is crucial with respect to ethical considerations and data protection concerns. And in practical terms, you will not want to be caught out with a high-quality recording of an exciting conversation that you cannot access or use.

Digital audio recorders

As the audio tracks are often the weakest element of the smartphone or tablet recordings, it may be necessary to consider purchasing a separate gadget. Digital audio recorders are available relatively cheaply, but are quite limited in their functions. Depending on the device, you may be able to record individual voices as separate tracks with individual microphones for each speaker. The advantage is obvious – individual tracks with clear speech recordings. However, that set-up is more expensive than a simple recording device that is reminiscent of the initial dictaphones. That said, the quality of dictaphones has increased drastically since their beginnings, and so may be sufficient for your purposes. If you are thinking about investing in a digital audio recorder for research journalling, you may want to consider other opportunities, such as recording conference presentations or podcasts. In that case, a dedicated recorder with different sets of microphones may be more suitable.

Most digital recording devices are sold in sets, and so it is quite helpful to know a little bit about microphones. In practice, microphones are an entire technological world of their own, but as a starting point it is worth considering your potential recording set-up to decide between cardioid or omnidirectional microphones. Cardioid microphones are unidirectional, which pick up the sounds coming from the front most sensitively, with the sounds from the sides being recorded less clearly. Omnidirectional microphones, by contrast, work in such a way that they record everything equally that happens around them. The difference lies with what you want to record. If you are after particular voices, then cardioid microphones for each individual would be the best set-up. If, however, you just want to capture the sounds as a soundscape in a cafe or bustling market, for example, then the omnidirectional microphone is more appropriate. Another consideration may be if you intend to record predominantly outdoors or indoors, as some microphones are better than others at reducing unwanted noises like those from wind or cars. Accessories are also available, such as microphone muffs and wind covers to facilitate the regulation of background noises. In addition, you will need some accessories, such as the relevant data cables and storage cards, and probably some form of case to transport everything in. Once you have everything packed up to go, you are carrying another kilogram of extra weight in a separate case. The question then is: will you be taking that extra bag or will you not bother? The quality of the recordings is genuinely great and really does not compare to the phone recordings, but you do need to decide whether this is worth the money and effort. As a starting point, I recommend you check out the Zoom audio recorders. Zoom is a very popular and long-lived brand offering a good variety of recorders for different purposes, from podcasting and recording music to film or media production in various price ranges. I own the Zoom H6 recorder with a set of four cardioid and omnidirectional microphones, muffs and wind cover. The initial investment was probably more than I would have wanted to spend on a recording device, but I am equipped for pretty much every recording situation, and I do use the recorder regularly.

Digital cameras and video recorders

With gadgets, the sky is the limit, and visual recording devices are no different. The choice is between heavier tools of higher quality with more functionalities that are more cumbersome to handle versus cheaper, slimmer, lighter, thinner gadgets with more limited functionalities that can easily fit into coat pockets, trouser pockets or small bags. In order to truly benefit from the more expensive tools, you need to learn to make the most out of the gadget in front of you. Often, people who own a sophisticated digital SLR camera are not particularly confident in using all its functions, as the process of learning to use the camera is overwhelming. If you do not want to fully commit to exploring a camera, then it may be better to settle for a cheaper, lightweight one that is capable of producing higher resolution photographs rather than owning a camera that produces lower resolution photographs as a trade-off for its intricate functionalities. I used to have my own point-and-shoot camera, but at some point, I decided to invest in a more expensive smartphone as I hardly ever had the camera on me when it mattered. However, my husband and son both have their own digital SLR cameras, and I do occasionally borrow theirs for recordings and photography projects. My issue with digital SLR cameras is that they do become quite heavy to hold over time, so I end up needing a tripod, which, to me, is just more gear that needs to be lugged around. In the comfort of our own home, in a studio or in someone else's home, though, the quality of pictures and the creative opportunities for photography are appealing.

I would like to mention here the GoPro action cameras. They are not the cheapest of devices available, and their functionalities are limited, but they do offer the kinds of recordings that other cameras cannot. GoPro cameras are specifically made for activities, and so have steadying methods in-built that ensure that the visuals do not jag too much. Additionally, there are options for capturing time lapses, which offer a particularly interesting tool for recording observations. In one of my research projects, I wanted to determine the rhythm of buildings, the ebb and flow of bodies navigating and occupying spaces (Brown and Morgan, 2021), and in this context the GoPro camera was particularly useful. The small device on a mini-tripod was not obtrusive, so that people did not change their ordinary behaviours, which they might have done with a bigger recording set-up. Implicit in this description is again the consideration of purpose and intentionality, which are, after all, the main factors for deciding which gadgets to use.

TRY THIS!

Play with the words from your readings

The next time you read a journal article or book relating to your research, try to take reading notes differently by creating a poem, playing with words or creating a word cloud from that article. Then reflect on what you have gained or lost through that activity.

Record differently

Imagine the two scenarios described below and consider what your data would be, how you would record that data in these different situations and which recording devices, templates or gadgets you would need. As a next step, reflect on what would happen if you were to change your recording strategy – which aspects or details of the recording would you gain or lose?

- Scenario 1: You are in a bustling market in Asia and your aim is to capture your observations. Once you have completed this task, you may want to check the work of Dawn Lyon (2016), which is a rhythmanalysis of Billingsgate Fish Market in London. As you watch her version of this task, you may want to reflect on whether you feel you are missing something and how you would be able to fill that gap.
- Scenario 2: You are researching educational settings and your aim is to record problem behaviours in a classroom. Once you have thought through this situation, you may want to read the chapter by Skinner et al (2000) where they provide an insight into thought processes relating to naturalistic observations in educational settings.

Journal your sensory experiences

One of the tasks in Chapter 3 was 'Train your senses', where you were asked to record in any way that felt comfortable what you observed, heard, felt or smelled. Building on this series of exercises, create different journal entries from those recordings. You may want to journal your sensory experiences by constructing a word cloud, by creating a poem or fictionalisation, or you may want to create an assemblage, collage or painting. Again, as you work through these different examples, consider what happens to your data and what you gain or lose in these forms of recording.

Go to https://policy.bristoluniversitypress.co.uk/making-the-most-of-your-research-journal/online-resources for:

- **A description of five different models of reflection**
- **The figures in full-sized format and colour**

5

When to record in a research journal?

Chapter aims

- To provide the context for good journalling habits.

- To outline how we can prepare and plan for when to record.

- To consider and remedy the trade-offs of not having recorded enough.

Introduction

One of the major deterrents for journalling is the felt pressure of needing to meet particular expectations around the research journal. This relates to every aspect of journalling, from the format, design and layout of the journal, to what is recorded, how entries are made and when journalling is to happen.

Advice from research handbooks or journalling guidebooks and templates like those commonly used in bullet journals often adds to this overwhelming feeling of pressure. Resources like these are a great starting point to learn about keeping research journals, but the issue is that the guidance is often very specific regarding its focus on writing, a particular way of maintaining journals and regularity of creating entries. One such example is the recommendation to journal every day and to provide deeper reflections three to five times a week. Such recommendations are clearly well intended, but not really helpful. These guidelines put us journallers under pressure to write an entry, when we may not have anything important or relevant to say. As a result, entries become forced, superficial and meaningless. At the same time, the guidelines set us journallers up for failure. We know that we are supposed to journal once a day quickly, and three to five times a week for a longer, more carefully planned session. If we miss a session or two or three entries, we feel like we are not meeting our targets and not doing our work. Consequently, we begin to associate the journal with negative feelings, which will inevitably lead to us abandoning the journalling process altogether. I write this part with full conviction without substantiating through references to literature, because I am writing from my own experience, but also others', like my colleagues', my friends' and my students'. If you have read this book chapter by chapter, you will by now have begun to recognise the main message regarding journalling: there are no rules, and the trajectory described earlier does not need to follow.

In this chapter, I discuss the practicalities of taking notes and recording thoughts and observations during the research process. Within notes-intensive studies such as ethnographies, narrative or interview studies in particular, we researchers are not able to record everything immediately. I thereby expand on the theme of making choices from Chapter 3, and highlight how to create the justification for and context of consistent note-taking.

Developing good habits

Before diving in to explore 'when to record' it is necessary to set up the context for the right frame of mind. In Chapter 3, the idea of a specific attitude towards journalling was introduced that asks for the journaller's openness, trust, playfulness, creativity and expectation of fun. Linked to the 'when to record' are the elements of openness and trust. We journallers need to be open to new developments and trusting when it comes to potentially changing existing habits and routines. Journalling cannot be expected to become automatised or natural if it is not occurring regularly enough for a habit to form. Behaviours are described as habitual if they are being 'performed frequently (at least twice a month) and extensively (at least 10 times)' (Ronis et al, 1988: 213). This suggests that creating two journal entries for 10 months in a row would make journalling a habitual behaviour. A study published by Lally et al (2010) in the *European Journal of Social Psychology* specifically explored the formation of habits and development of routines. The authors found that while the automatisation of habits and behaviours occurred on average after around 66 days of daily engagement, the range recorded among the research participants was between 18 and 254 days. When the authors compared the changes relating to simple behaviours with changes regarding more complex behaviours, they found that the complex behaviours required one-and-a-half times more time. Leaving aside the discussion of whether journalling is to be considered a simple or complex behaviour, it becomes obvious that getting used to journalling will take time. In fact, 'within psychology "habits" are defined as actions that are triggered automatically in response to contextual cues' (Gardner et al, 2012: 664). For example, getting into a car and putting the seat belt on or washing your hands after having been to the toilet are such automatic, triggered responses to the contextual cues. Journalling, then, would only be considered a habit if you were automatically journalling in response to picking up a pen or switching on the computer.

Let us be realistic here: this is not going to happen. It is not my intention to add more pressure, anxiety or worry, but I do think it is important to be realistic about expectations. Even if journalling is experienced as more manageable and fun, at least sometimes, this does not necessarily make the process an automatic behaviour. We may need to invest time and effort for longer before we can consider ourselves habitual journallers.

Scheduling times for journalling

To facilitate the process of developing a journalling habit, for journalling to become second nature, and for there to be sufficient time for journalling, scheduling specific times may be helpful. You can set yourself the target to journal for 15 minutes each day. If you find you do not have anything to journal about, then journal about that. The aim is not to produce a coherent journal entry, but to get into the routine of journalling regularly and to develop good writing habits (Jensen, 2017). Instead of journalling daily, another strategy is to carve out longer periods of time for journalling once or twice a week. You may want to add an entry in your diary or calendar to block out 30 or 40 minutes every Monday at 2 in the afternoon and Thursdays at 9 in the morning, for example. This means that nobody can ask you for meetings in that time, and you have your space and time carved out.

The risk with scheduled times is that you may not feel you have anything of relevance to add to your journal entry and more often than not you may end up journalling about not wanting to journal. For many journallers, therefore, building journalling times into everyday activities is more beneficial than organising set days or times in the diary. If on waking up your first action of the day or your last action of the day at bedtime is to reach for your phone to catch up on messages, emails, news or social media posts, then maybe building in time for an electronic entry relating to the to-do list in your research journal does not feel too peculiar. Equally, if there is a time in the day, week or month where you are catching up with administrative tasks of bills or other paperwork, adding another 10 or 20 minutes for dealing with research expenses in the finance tracker again may not feel too disruptive.

What is implied, but needs to be made explicit here, is that there is no need to attend to all the different elements and tasks of the research journal at once at all times. A to-do list will probably need to be dealt with more regularly than the finance tracker or the research pipeline. Some of the trackers, such as the ideas boxes or the achievements records, are only relevant at particular points within the research life. Similarly, particular kinds of activities in the research process, such as data collection or analysis, will more naturally call for further engagement with the research journal than others, such as writing up findings or disseminating results. As a consequence, journalling can actually never be a fully consistent, regular endeavour, but one that follows the natural ebb and flow of the research process as well as working life more generally. In this sense, the assumption that having fixed scheduled times can ever be suitable appears ludicrous. Instead, it may be more realistic to organise 'semi-scheduled' times for journalling.

I focus here on what was called 'journalling from the field' in Chapter 3, where I introduced three different categories of journal entries: observations and conversations, emotions and experiences, and thoughts and reflections, which largely relate to the data collection and analysis phases of the research process. If you know that you will be carrying out an observation or interview, you may be able to schedule additional times before and after the data collection event to ensure you have time to also record your thoughts or emotions. That is why, for want of a better word, I use the term 'semi-scheduled' to emphasise the fact that journalling does need to be built into the research process, while there does not have to be a fixed day or time.

For some scholars, research and practice go hand in hand and cannot be separated one from one another, so the process of reflecting and recording those reflections is happening simultaneously as the practice of research itself (Candy, 2011). Most commonly, this is the case for scholars from creative disciplines, such as fine arts or media production, but also for academics from contexts such as nursing, counselling and education, where reflection-in-action and reflection-on-action (Schön, 1987) are integral to everyday, professional practice.

To alleviate the pressures of needing to record everything now, it may make sense to have what Kara (2015) calls a 'reflexivity plan', a schedule with particular focus points in the research process where you will stop to think. Although Kara's plan focuses on reflexivity and answering reflexive questions, that wider schedule or plan is equally relevant to all journalling from the field. For example, as you schedule interviews and observations, you may want to plan a stop-think-record opportunity for when you have collected the equivalent of 5 or 10 hours of data. At that stage, you will have relevant information and thoughts to go on to make the journalling worthwhile and meaningful, and you are also able to capture your experiences with relative authenticity and immediacy. If you have journalled before and after each interview, you may want to schedule that stop-think-record opportunity after having collected the equivalent of 5 or 10 hours of data to revisit your previous journal entries (see Chapter 6 for what to do with the journal entries). This broader plan is probably more easily attainable, as it can also be tied in with the target tracker or to-do list.

In relation to the more creative elements of journalling, you may find that you will get to them as and when you are in the right frame of mind and mood. Of course, you can schedule an opportunity to create poetry at a particular point, such as after having carried out 20 interviews or after having read five scholarly articles. In reality, however, creativity cannot be forced. Contrary to popular belief, creative ideas do not necessarily fly under time pressures. The relationship between time pressures and creative thinking is more complex and depends on how determined individuals feel about their tasks (Amabile et al, 2002) and the working environment they find themselves in (Amabile et al, 1996). Generally, we are more creative, the more passionate we are about the task in hand, the less pressurised we feel from external sources, the safer we feel to give honest, constructive feedback and the more comfortable we are in sharing our thoughts with others (Amabile and Fisher, 2009).

In short, you can schedule 'a creative hour' or 'playtime', but you cannot go to that scheduled hour or playtime with a particular expectation regarding an outcome. Instead, consider this as your time to externalise what is happening in and around you. Enjoy it and have fun. There will be other times where you feel compelled to write a journal entry, play with words or create a collage, which will be with a specific aim in mind, but these are most likely to happen unscheduled.

From unscheduled to expected journalling

The biggest frustration in the earlier stages of my research career was that the best ideas always hit when I was not prepared. I would be driving my son to school, enjoying a long soak in the bath, be in the middle of a grocery shop or find myself in this semi-conscious, semi-dreamy state of light sleep, when an exciting idea or fantastic wording for writing popped into my mind. In most of these situations, of course, I was not able to use my computer, did not have my journal on me, or any other scrap paper and pen. By the time I did get organised enough to be able to record my thoughts or phrases, they were no longer as strong or as good because they had started to drift out of my mind. There were occasions when I got up in the middle of the night, jumped out of the bathtub or pulled over on the main road, but this was not a long-term solution. I needed to find a way to be prepared and expect these unscheduled opportunities for journalling.

From historical and anecdotal sources, we know that many creative thinkers were regular walkers spending time outdoors: Charles Darwin, William Wordsworth, Ludwig van Beethoven, Samuel T. Coleridge, Charles Dickens, Friedrich Nietzsche and Henry David Thoreau are just some names that spring to mind (Gros, 2014). For Wordsworth, focusing attention on perception and experience turned walking into a poetic activity to such an extent that he even considered walkers as silent poets (Gaillet-De Chezelles, 2010). This is not a coincidence. Scholarly research proves time and again the significant connection of the mind with the body when walking (Lambourne and Tomporowski, 2010). The relationship between walking and enhanced creativity lies in the circulatory and chemical changes due to the physical act of walking along with improved moods that these physiological changes bring (Oppezzo and Schwartz, 2014). In simple terms, the physical act of walking demands a particular cognitive load that works as a distraction and frees up the mind. The side effect of this distraction is that creativity can seep in. Further and more detailed experiments found that nature and the natural environment are conducive to increasing cognitive control and that they improve thinking (Berman et al, 2008). What exactly it is about nature that affects human minds in this way is not proven, but may be due to nature's peacefulness combined with the distraction and diversion of attention it offers.

Knowing about and being consciously aware of these connections is a first step towards what may seem paradoxical: planning for the unexpected. If you know that being in the outdoors and being distracted from your research tasks through walking results in creative surges, take advantage of that and treat walking as that active idleness it is often described as (O'Mara, 2020). First, start incorporating activities like walks into your everyday schedule. You may not be able to walk for several hours at a time, like Coleridge or Beethoven did, but you may fit in a fast-paced 20-minute walk between meetings or a short stroll in the garden, local housing estate or park. Second, approach walking with the right attitude, an attitude of purposeful openness. Let us assume, for example, you are in the process of writing for publication and you are stuck with your argument or the structure of that article. This is where the intentional walk can come in useful. You cannot expect to find solutions to problems if you are not prepared or do not have relevant information or background knowledge. In the scenario described, however, your walk has a purpose – to find a solution to the issue. As you go on your walk, be open to the prospect of possibly, but not necessarily, solving that problem: 'Walk for the enjoyment of walking, and for the enjoyment of thinking about the problem' (O'Mara, 2020: 164). And third, you can be prepared for the moment where the solution comes to you by having some recording tools on you. Shane O'Mara describes how he uses a dictaphone to talk into and record his texts while he walks, but we also know that Coleridge, Darwin and Dickens kept notebooks and pens or pencils on them as they went on their walks. In today's age the smartphone is probably the most obvious answer, as it is possible to record audio tracks, type notes and add images or videos from the walk, too.

It is a privilege to have the time, opportunity and mobility to take a break and go for a walk safely, and it may be that you have to find your personal alternative for what has been proposed here. For example, Sonia Overall (2021) offers exercises to tap into the power of walking that can be practised in the comfort of your own home or that may be rescaled and adapted accordingly in her book *walk write (repeat)*. By planning for the unexpected, it is almost possible to manufacture the conditions that are conducive to creative thinking for the purpose of journalling. Of course, there are still occasions when creativity and inspiration happen at entirely unscheduled times, but for me, they are no longer unexpected, and I am no longer unprepared. I take my phone everywhere, and when I have an idea, I journal immediately. This journalling may consist of bullet points, single words and simple phrases, or it may turn into a fully formulated paragraph. As always, there are choices to be made and trade-offs to be taken into account.

Journalling means making choices

Where I discussed what to record and how (Chapters 3 and 4), I hinted at the fact that researchers are not able to record everything immediately. It is sometimes not possible to know what will be relevant at a later stage. At the same time, however, it is counterproductive to try and capture everything, as we would end up like the holidaymakers with their cameras who experience their vacation by looking at the photographs after the fact rather than in the moment. Instead, we should have confidence and trust in the choices we make about what we record at the time, even if this may mean not having some details later on. After all, there are ways to remedy the issue once we have identified that we missed something important.

Notes and annotations

Drawing once more on the categories presented in Chapter 3, notes and annotations are particularly suited to capture additional information, such as emotions and experiences, thoughts and reflections. In the middle of journalling, we may easily overlook important connections, which can be remedied with the passage of time and the benefit of hindsight. Sometimes, the temporal distance to previous notes on observations and conversations may have also helped us develop deeper understanding through additional reading. Journalling in the form of adding notes and annotating existing entries therefore offers the opportunity to delve further into relevant matters and analyses.

Lesley Price, whose target tracker was presented in Chapter 3, uses annotations to extremely good effect. In the first instance, she makes reading notes, taking particular care to meticulously record the bibliographic information of her sources. At a later point in time, she revisits her original notes, and adds questions, comments and analytical reflections by scribbling into gaps (see Figure 5.1).

Although this is not visible in this photograph, Lesley also applies a system of cross-referencing in her journal. If, for example, she

Figure 5.1: Lesley Price's reading notes and annotations

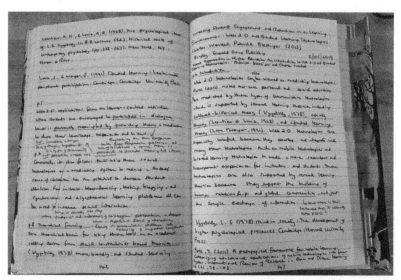

would like to add more notes and annotations on a page than she has space for, she continues her analytical reflections on a new page within the same journal, but links back to this page by referring to the relevant page number in her journal. In fact, Lesley cross-references all her notebooks in this way. Her journal entries therefore become a collection of critical, analytical records, which can easily be incorporated within the more polished and accomplished writing of journal articles or reports.

Vignettes and critical incidents as journal entries

Critical incidents (Tripp, 1993) and vignettes (Lieberman, 1987) have long been recognised tools in qualitative research to support data collection, analysis and/or dissemination. Vignettes and critical incidents are applied regularly across the globe in the social sciences, but specifically in disciplines related to nursing, education or social work (Hughes and Huby, 2002). Although there is no consistency regarding terminology, with literature using 'scenarios' alongside 'vignettes' (Bradbury-Jones et al, 2014), for example, the basic principles are the same. Relevant situations and events are identified or created and practitioners or research participants are asked to respond to these scenarios (Renold, 2002) or descriptive accounts (Richman and Mercer, 2002). Writing critical incidents or creating vignettes ensures journalling and note-taking are consistent, systematic and purposeful, even after a considerable amount of time has passed.

The aim of the critical incidents and vignettes is to capture a reality of scenarios as they have or may have happened. Scenarios are therefore constructed based on data sources ranging from experiences and memories to literature, with a particular level of authenticity covering fully real cases as well as fully hypothetical events (Bradbury-Jones et al, 2014). The difference between critical incidents and vignettes probably lies in the amount of fictionalisation involved in the process of writing up the scenarios, with critical incidents largely drawing on memories of real events, while vignettes are intentional creations with specific purposes. These wide ranges of possibilities for the vignette and critical incident construction hint at the main critiques of using such an approach in qualitative research: a critique relating to the validity, relevance and realism of the cases constructed (Hughes and Huby, 2012). Yet, with the proviso that as journallers we intend to capture our reality of an important event, the creation of vignettes and critical incidents offers opportunities for subsequent sense-making processes (Skilling and Stylianides, 2020).

For critical incidents and vignettes to become systematic entries in the research journal, some foundational contents need to be covered. The following (Figure 5.2) was developed and adapted from Ann Lieberman (1987: 6).

Figure 5.2: Nicole Brown's vignette template

Context	Note a little bit about the context you refer to in your vignette.
My intentions/ hopes	Explain what your intentions were or what you hoped would happen.
Who was involved?	Describe if you were on your own or with other people.
What did I do? What did others do?	Write out what you did and what others did.
What happened? What was the impact?	Make a note of the consequences of the actions, yours and others'. This section may also include reflections, thoughts and feelings.
Why did that happen?	Theorise the experience. You may want to draw on literature here to make sense systematically.
Other comments	Keep a record of anything else that you consider important. For example, you may want to link to other vignettes or critical incidents, or you may want to note how you will follow up this experience with further readings.

Source: Template developed by drawing on Lieberman (1987: 6)

Go to https://policy.bristoluniversitypress.co.uk/making-the-most-of-your-research-journal/online-resources to download a vignette template. It outlines key areas that may be considered when creating a vignette or critical incident. The 'critical' element of the incidents described is not about seriousness or danger; it relates to the profoundness of experiences.

In some instances, not all of the sections will be relevant; in others, you may find yourself writing detailed descriptions and analyses. It is important to remember that, ultimately, there are no rules regarding the length or depth of descriptions. Instead, the entry in the research journal needs to work for you.

The following extract (see Figure 5.3) is from my own journal, where the page has a two-third and one-third split for annotations. This first of a series of pages covering critical incidents and stories relating to hearing loss, dealings with hearing aids and situations

Figure 5.3: Nicole Brown's critical incident

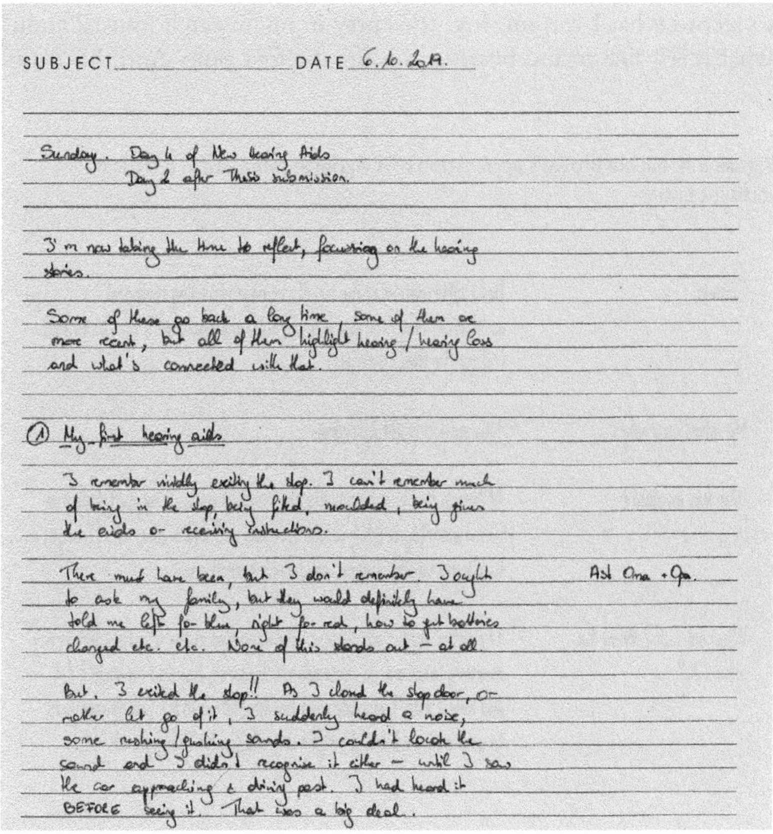

SUBJECT_____ DATE 6.10.2019.

Sunday. Day 4 of New hearing Aids
      Day 2 after Thesis submission.

I'm now taking the time to reflect, focussing on the hearing
stories.

Some of these go back a long time, some of them are
more recent, but all of them highlight hearing / hearing loss
and what's connected with that.

① My first hearing aids

I remember vividly exactly the shop. I can't remember much
of being in the shop, being fitted, moulded, being given
the aids or receiving instructions.

There must have been, but I don't remember. I ought   Ask Oma + Opa
to ask my family, but they would definitely have
told me left for them, right for red, how to get batteries
charged etc. etc. None of this stands out – at all.

But. I exited the shop!! As I closed the shop door, or
rather let go of it, I suddenly heard a noise,
some rushing / pushing sounds. I couldn't locate the
sound and I didn't recognise it either – until I saw
the car approaching & driving past. I had heard it
BEFORE seeing it! That was a big deal.

revolving audiology matters is a typical example of record-taking after the fact. The first incident described on this page refers to an event that had occurred in 1986 or 1987, thus some 30-odd years before the entry in my research journal. At the time of the event, I was around 10 or 11 years old, and even if I had kept diaries at that stage of my life, I would certainly not have written about getting hearing aids. The process of journalling about that event therefore was to tap into memories.

Note in Figure 5.4 how the template presented earlier is applied in this journal entry.

The next three sections ('What happened?', 'What was the impact?, Why did that happen?' and 'Other comments') are not included in this entry, as the theorisation of the experiences happened in later entries in my research journal. There is more about what to do with journal entries in Chapter 6, but suffice it to say here, there is no obligation to cover all aspects of a template at once. Instead, the entry needs to reflect the purpose of writing. The purpose of my entry here was not to theorise experiences or to make sense of behaviours; it was merely to record what I was missing: the entry in my research journal about what it felt like to use hearing aids for the first time. And this is my

Figure 5.4: Nicole Brown's application of a vignette template in a critical incident entry

Context	Brief information at the top of the page providing temporal association (day 4 of new hearing aids) and framework for the entries (taking the time to reflect).
My intentions/hopes	This section is not described.
Who was involved?	Although this is not explicitly described, there is an implicit depiction of the audiologist (they would have told me) and my parents (I ought to ask my family; annotation) having been there.
What did I do? What did others do?	The entry implies what must have happened in the situation, but as my memory failed me on these counts, I merely focussed on what I did and how I felt. I also included the annotation to ask family members to gain a more detailed insight into what actually happened.

key message from this section: applying critical incidents or vignettes as strategies for recording enables you to catch up with what you may have missed in the field.

Immediacy and authenticity

In the context of ethnographic and anthropological fieldnotes, journallers are particularly concerned with issues of immediacy and authenticity. A commonly used argument is that journalling needs to happen immediately for the records to be authentic and to reflect that authenticity. This is because as journallers we rely on our memories, and the more removed we are from the events in temporality, the more inaccurate or distorted our recollection will become (Atkinson, 2020). The reality is somewhat more nuanced.

In *Writing Ethnographic Fieldnotes* Robert Emerson et al (2011) distinguish between different kinds of writing: from jottings and fieldnotes created at the desk from those jottings, to analytical documents and the final ethnographically produced texts for dissemination purposes. Jottings are explained as a writing activity to facilitate fully formulated, thick descriptions that are 'written close to or even in the immediate presence of those whose words and deeds are at issue' (Emerson et al, 2011: 34f). Recognising the tension between authenticity and intrusion, the authors specifically highlight that there is a choice to be made about jottings in the field:

> Clearly, looking down to pad or keyboard to write jottings distracts the field researcher (even if only momentarily), making close and continuous observation of what may be complex, rapid, and subtle actions by others very difficult. But beyond limited attention, jotting decisions can have tremendous import for relations with those in the field. The researcher works hard to establish close ties with participants so that she may be included in activities that are central to their lives. In the midst of such activities, however, she may experience deep ambivalence: On the one hand, she may wish to preserve the immediacy of the moment by jotting down words as they are spoken and details of scenes as they are enacted, while, on the other hand, she may feel that taking out a notepad or smartphone will ruin the moment and plant seeds of distrust. Participants may now see her as someone whose primary interest lies in discovering their secrets and turning their most intimate and cherished

> experiences into objects of scientific inquiry. (Emerson
> et al, 2011: 35f)

Unfortunately, the tension is not resolved, and probably can never be fully resolved. The argument regarding the relationship between time and accuracy certainly stands, but for researchers in the field there are many variables that need to be taken into account: the circumstances and settings of the research, the relationships with the people in the field, and the purposes of journalling. In practice, what may be lost in terms of raw authenticity may be gained in depth of reflective and analytical understanding. This is where the arts-based approach of journalling may be particularly beneficial, as the artistic, creative expression taps into the intuitive and authentic. By engaging with creative expression through painting, collage, model-making or any other form of doing and making art or craft, we can connect our critical, reflective analysis with experiences.

I would like to add some final considerations as food for thought to the matters of immediacy and authenticity. Experiences can indeed be journalled as rawer, more authentic entries the closer they are to the experiences because memories are distorted and inaccurate. However, just because memories are distorted through the lens of time, the feelings, experiences or memories are no less true. Let us consider the critical incident from the hearing aid shop presented earlier in this chapter as an example. When I journalled about that critical incident, I was fully aware of the limitations of my memories. In fact, the entry itself highlights how much I had forgotten. Yet, at the same time, the memory of exiting the shop and hearing a car before seeing it for the first time was, and still is, so powerfully etched into my mind *and* body that I struggle to comprehend how the experience could ever be considered as invalid because of the inaccuracies. I know that through the temporal distortion of my memories the experience may have been shaped, constructed and reconstructed, but that should not make it any less true or less truthful. Under that proviso, can we therefore not accept these entries for what they are?

TRY THIS!

Annotate previous notes

You will already have been keeping some records and created some form of research journal. Take a random page or entry from your current research journal and make a working copy to add notes and annotate the entry. If you use a digitally saved copy, you may want to save that copy under a new name. If you use a pen-and-paper-type entry, I recommend you make a photocopy or photograph. Whichever way you work, just make sure you keep the original entry separate from this exercise. Using the comments function, the photography mark-up function or simply using different coloured pens, add your thoughts and reflections to your original entry. Consider what you gain from revisiting your previous notes. Reflect on how revisiting may shape your current understanding, and vice versa, how your current understanding may change the emphasis or focus of your previous work.

Vignette of your sensory experiences

One of the tasks in Chapter 3 was 'Train your senses', where you were asked to record in any way that felt comfortable what you observed, heard, felt or smelled. Building on this series of exercises, create a vignette and a critical incident of your observations. As you work through these two examples, consider what happens to your data and what you gain or lose in these forms of recording.

Experiment on your think-walks

The next time you feel your concentration starts to wane or you are stuck with a particular issue during your research work, go on a think-walk without any particular expectations. Make sure you have different recording tools on you to experiment with what works for you: smartphone, pen and paper, journal, notepad, dictaphone, camera, and the like. Be sensible about where you walk, make sure you are safe, and let friends or family know where you will be and how long you will be gone for. Depending on where you live, your think-walk may not be the natural environment of Coleridge's or Wordsworth's unblemished, rugged English countryside, but when you are out and about, note the surface you are walking on, be conscious of what the air feels like, consciously enjoy whatever your views are. Look at the sky, trees or bushes, see if you can spot some wildlife. And enjoy thinking.

Go to https://policy.bristoluniversitypress.co.uk/making-the-most-of-your-research-journal/online-resources for:

- **A vignette template**
- **Application of a vignette template**
- **The figures in full-sized format and colour**

6

What to do with the journal entries?

Chapter aims

- To demonstrate that research journalling is a sense-making process.
- To outline how research journalling may be used for dissemination purposes.
- To consider research journalling as an iterative, cyclical activity.

Introduction

Maintaining an effective research journal consistently and efficiently is hard enough and often not talked about or taught. Within the traditions and conventions of ethnography, fieldnotes are a substantive element of the process, and are genuinely used purposefully to create a particular end product. In most other disciplines, however, journalling and journal entries are not shared. Somehow and somewhere in the process of being advised or made to keep a journal it is just assumed that we all know what we are supposed to do with our entries. Academic writing guidance and workshops focus on getting people to write regularly to become more proficient at formulating arguments. In an effort to improve practical writing skills and knowledge, it seems the practicality of dealing with the entries from journalling is neglected or ignored. Yet, if we spend so much time and energy on journalling and recording details, then surely we ought to do something purposeful and meaningful with those entries.

Let me remind you of two journalling principles mentioned elsewhere in this book: (1) anything and everything goes, and (2) tools and contexts need to fit the purpose. These principles also apply in relation to what to do with the journal and its entries. There are no limits, other than perhaps our lack of imagination, sense of adventure or flexibility. Naturally, within the context of academic careers and publishing, there may be conventions that we do need to adhere to, and where particular kinds of output are perhaps not considered as scholarly enough, or as too innovative or too risky (see Chapter 6 in Leigh and Brown, 2021). However, you can decide to be that marathon runner in the wetsuit aiming at breaking different kinds of records. If you feel strongly about your way of working and that way of working is not commonly accepted in your usual dissemination haunts, then consider different contexts, settings, tools or vehicles for dissemination. The secret, if it is one, is not to shape your work to fit other people's purposes, but to find your place and your people, even if this is sometimes difficult (Brown, 2019a). Ultimately, what you do in and with your journalling is always about fitness for purpose.

What follows in the remainder of this chapter is an outline of using journals with three different purposes and contexts in mind: using journal entries as a way to provide evidence, developing journal entries to make sense of experiences and previous knowledge, and using journal entries to share your research with a greater variety of audiences.

Using journal entries to provide evidence

Although the idea of using journal entries to provide evidence may be stark, the fact is that the journalling is meant to capture observations and conversations, emotions and experiences, thoughts and reflections. These journal entries are there as an opportunity to learn from and interact with. The initial notes are:

> liminal, intermediate texts ... between the personal experience of fieldwork and the less personal analysis of social forms and processes of action. (Atkinson, 2020: 48)

Yet, by committing these thoughts and observations onto paper, they become data that we can interact with. To this end, Robert Burgess (1981) recommends journalling with three emphases in mind. In our substantive accounts, we should provide a detailed chronological record of what has happened, while the methodological account should provide details of the research process and our position as researchers within that process. Burgess's interpretation of a methodological account also includes reflexive content and information about how data analysis is approached in theory. The analytic account itself is then a continuous record of concepts applied and questions raised to analyse data in practice, especially as participants may provide analytical insights and glimpses of interpretation, which we journallers will follow up on. Meticulously kept journal entries are therefore evidence of our personal, professional and intellectual development and of the conclusions we draw in our analyses.

Being able to draw on such detailed evidence is not only useful within the scope of dissemination or providing context for publications, but also regarding matters of academic integrity. Academic integrity encompasses research ethics as well as the wide array of academic misconduct including fraud, cheating, plagiarism, deceit, impropriety, falsification or infringements of intellectual property (Decoo, 2001). It does not matter how misconduct is defined in detail or how academic integrity has been breached. What does matter is that in such cases the onus of providing evidence often lies with the person who has been accused of misconduct. In Chapter 5, in a somewhat different context, I mentioned the role and relevance of memories. Yet, in connection with misconduct panels, memories and recollections of conversations are not considered as sufficient and substantial evidence, whereas journal entries are. In no way am I suggesting here that you will be caught up in a case of misconduct. I am merely suggesting that good record-keeping may come in handy if you need to show that you have not falsified experiment results, or if you ever need to prove that you had an idea before someone else published it.

Making sense through journal entries

In Chapters 3, 4 and 5 I have shown how to journal, when and what about, and what should have emerged from these sections is that journalling is a process of making sense. First, the action of writing or creating and committing something to a journal is making sense through that process of doing. Second, reflecting on initial journal entries, annotating and adding further ideas deepens that initial sense-making. And third, engaging with the journal entries by experimenting with different means of expression or communication or by systematically incorporating literature, for example, allows for analysis, theorisation and conceptualisation. In practice, revisiting journal entries leads us journallers to reconsider our experiences. This reconsideration, in turn, supports processes of reflection and introspection. Consequently, we are able to arrive at a much deeper understanding of the situations on hand (Friedemann et al, 2011).

Revisiting journal entries is in itself a form of journalling and, like the original journalling process, should be systematic and purposeful.

Sometimes the purpose of revisiting a journal or specific entries may simply be finding out about previous experiences and states of mind with no intention of gaining additional information or insights. In Act 2 of *The Importance of Being Earnest*, Oscar Wilde famously justified not travelling without a diary because 'one should always have something sensational to read'. This is certainly true, and if you revisit your journal in that way, you are still revisiting it purposefully. In most instances, revisiting the journal will have a more particular function related to your research work.

Analysis

Probably the most important reason for revisiting journal entries is to develop analysis, conceptualisation and theorisation. The image of Lesley Price's journal in Chapter 5 is one such example where Lesley had revisited previous reading notes to add deeper thoughts in her annotations. Annotating is only one form of analysis. Another form of analytical development is described in Chapter 4 within the context of journalling with models of reflection, in creative writing tasks or through arts-based approaches, as in the images from my journals and Aine McAllister's.

What has been neglected so far, however, is the formal process of analysing such as by coding for a thematic analysis (Braun and Clarke, 2006, 2019) or by employing visual analysis (Rose, 2016). Whatever your theoretical framework is, the likelihood is that there is no rule stating you cannot use your own journal entries as data. Indeed, even very specific frameworks such as Interpretative Phenomenological Analysis (Smith et al, 2012), which is particularly tight in its rules and guidelines, demand a consideration of the researcher's positionality. Although considering positionality is not the same as coding, there is nothing in the rules of Interpretative Phenomenological Analysis that would stop us from treating our own journal entries like another participant's data, and therefore subjecting them to our coding process. As there is tension around immediacy and authenticity during journalling, there is tension relating to the connection with the entry. So, depending on the temporal and emotional proximity between our entry and our coding, the analytical process may be quite straightforward or could be problematic. There is clearly a choice to be made between the costs and benefit of dealing with our own entries. On the one hand, we may gain significant insights that will help us identify further theoretical principles. On the other hand, we may not feel comfortable revisiting specific kinds of entries because we are not emotionally distanced enough from our own experiences. I, myself, have journal entries across my many completed and abandoned journals that I never revisit. Let me say this: there is no rule stopping you from coding your journal entries, and there is also no rule forcing you to do so.

Whichever choice you make, coding all your entries or only some of them, not coding them at all but using them for creative, analytical developments, there are three criteria you need to account for: criticality, transparency and reflexivity (Brown, 2019b, c: 497, 2020). First, you need to critically engage with research and its methods, the data and their interpretation, and the choices that you and/or your participants make and to critically view and review individual stages in a reflective and reflexive cycle, to look for different, potentially opposing views or interpretations. Second, you need to be transparent, open and honest about the choices you make and why. And third, you need to be transparent about your own self, and thus think reflexively about your biases, prejudices and world views to recognise where and how you shape your data and analysis. These three principles, criticality, transparency and reflexivity, are interconnected facets of the same concern within the motto of 'anything and everything goes', and only by meeting these criteria is it possible to do anything and everything.

Reflexivity

Probably the most common use for research journals and their entries is the development of a reflexivity statement. Although the definition of reflexivity is somewhat vague, especially once it is considered in relation to reflection and reflective practice (D'Cruz et al, 2007), a common working understanding has evolved of what reflexivity looks like in research. Reflexivity is an attitude of examining one's frameworks of thought and systematically attending to knowledge construction and the researcher's role within that (May and Perry, 2017). 'Doing' reflexivity therefore means to not take things for granted, but to challenge them through second-order questioning (Kara, 2015), which is where the journal entries come in. At particular times throughout the process of research and writing up, journallers revisit journal entries to examine the recorded thoughts and emotions. The process is not dissimilar to the analytical reading of journal entries described above, but rather than employing a specific framework for data analysis, we journallers read our entries through a particular lens. The focus is on identifying which principles, frameworks of thought or biases underlie the journal entries. The findings from that interpretative reading are then used to formulate a reflexivity statement.

How deeply we engage with reflexivity and what reflexivity statements look like depend on disciplinary conventions as well as personal preferences. For some journallers, it may feel natural to write ourselves into our research, whereas others may fear repercussions from putting our flaws into the public arena (Smith, 2006). In fact, the ethnographer and anthropologist Sara Delamont, who has written extensively about approaches to qualitative research and issues of the self in research, warns against being too open and too self-revealing. Delamont (2018) argues that researchers, especially early career researchers, need to be trained or guided regarding developing reflexivity statements, just like we teach young adults about their use of social media. Like the unwanted photos of drunken escapades, any 'admission' made in a reflexivity statement may come back to haunt us at the most inopportune times. This does not mean that reflexive journal entries cannot be associated with confession or catharsis (Pillow, 2003). It merely means that not everything from the journal entries needs to be, or indeed should be, shared. The personal and private journal entries are only the basis for the public reflexivity statement.

Researcher wellbeing

The benefit of journalling as a space to offload ideas and thoughts for later was mentioned in Chapter 3. I used the term 'brain dump' in relation to to-do lists and trackers. However, journalling also means to have a dumping ground for emotional baggage. Writing journal entries is experienced as gratifying or cathartic (Friedemann et al, 2011) and considered a relief (Beale et al, 2004), as experiences are externalised and emotions verbalised in writing. Through these externalising and verbalising processes, feelings are written out of our system and our bodies, which results in significant reduction of trauma and stress (Stevens and Cooper, 2009). Joli Jensen (2017) recommends creating a separate journal for the specific purpose of venting and offloading unwanted thoughts of inadequacy or unhappiness, and calls this her 'ventilation file':

> This file offers me a confidential space for every hostile, resentful, negative thing that I think and feel.... The ventilation file is a nonjudgmental arena to express the doubts and fears. (Jensen, 2017: 18f)

Jensen goes on to explain that there is no particular need to revisit these kinds of entries, and that they can even be torn up. The principle of her ventilation file is simply to externalise and verbalise. I agree with the arguments of externalising and verbalising experiences and not needing to revisit journal entries. However, I do think that we should refrain from tearing up, shredding or otherwise disposing of our entries so that we can revisit them. It does not mean that we have to revisit those entries, but the revisiting remains an option.

The reason you may want to revisit 'emotion dump' entries is for your personal development and as a self-care routine to maintain mental and emotional wellbeing. Just as the journalling process is experienced as healing and cathartic, so is the revisiting, because it offers insights into your own being and state of mind, it provides opportunities to make sense of past experiences, and it evidences your trajectory and development. When we are in the thick of stressful situations or have received critical feedback, we tend to respond emotionally, focusing on the negatives. Revisiting an entry journalled at such an intensive time enables us to rationalise. Passage of time and hindsight provide the distance needed to process what has happened and to learn from that experience. There is no obligation to revisit all entries all of the time. As I said earlier, I also have entries I cannot bring myself to read. Yet I know that they are there, if ever I would want to and felt ready to as part of my self-care routine.

From making sense to sharing

In addition to using journal entries as evidence or for sense-making purposes, the entries can be used for dissemination. In fact, the boundaries between making sense and disseminating are oddly often blurred, as the process of developing shareable resources is anchored in and related to sense-making. With that in mind, it is entirely up to you how you revisit your entries and what you do with them: pure sense-making or sense-making with dissemination or pure dissemination. You do need to attend to the three criteria of good quality in research and consider the concerns relating to oversharing details. Instead of sharing the full journal entries, you may simply use them to draw on as you create what you are able and willing to share publicly.

Resources for teaching, research and practice

A very practical reason for revisiting and using your journal entries is to develop resources. To this end, you may want to reconsider entries in your ideas tracker, although journal entries that are 'emotion dumps' may also be helpful, as, for example, you are bemoaning the fact that what you need as a resource is not available. Revisiting journal entries with that specific view means you draw on evidence and work with or from experience. The large majority of the prompts, suggestions, strategies and techniques presented in this book come out of my own experiments with journalling.

In previous chapters, I presented creative approaches to journalling, and I would like to return to these as examples for what to do with these unconventional journal entries. Let us consider the soundscape from a cafe or the time lapse from a building. These recordings can be revisited for analytical or sense-making purposes as they are data after all. However, there is also an opportunity to use such recordings for dissemination purposes. Despite the fact that audiences will know what buildings look like or cafes sound like, they will not be familiar with the particular lens through which you have made your recording. Sharing a soundscape or video therefore affords you the luxury of sharing your experiences and teaching your audience about your learning. Naturally, you need to pay attention to ethical considerations regarding which materials you share and how, so you do not put people at risk and continue to ensure their anonymity (see Chapter 7). But even if materials are edited, the presentations where I get to see actual visual or auditory data are always the most notable and powerful, and the ones that stay with me long after the fact.

Graphic novel

The following (Figures 6.1 and 6.2) is a particularly exciting example of what to do with recordings from the field. Jason Wragg works as a lecturer at the University of Central Lancashire, with specific expertise in outdoor adventure leadership, adventure travel and adventure studies. In his research, Jason investigates and explores the lived experiences of adventure travel, specifically by motorcycle. Set within the overall voyage of the research are fieldwork journeys by motorcycle that are used to capture and record stories of the lived experience as well as to employ autoethnographic principles with a narrative methodology. While in the field Jason recorded observations, notes of conversations and details of the day's events, often supported by video and photographs along with more personal records of thoughts, feelings and considerations that were made at the time but are often supported by comments after the event when reflecting and looking back at the fieldwork. These notes brought together were

Figure 6.1: Jason Wragg's sketch script page

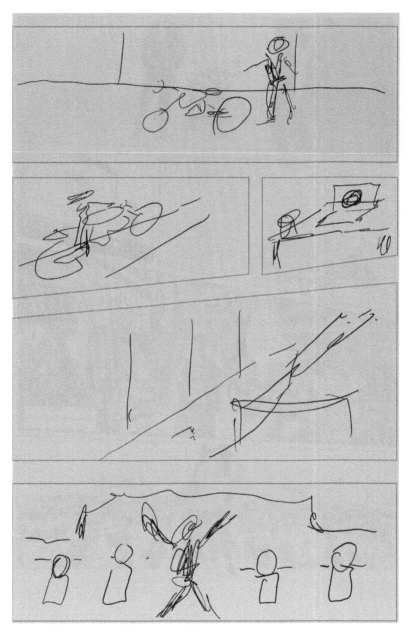

then used to create a graphic narrative, for which Jason worked with an artist to help him develop his rudimentary ideas and sketches into an accomplished graphic novel.

Figure 6.2: Jason Wragg's page as completed by Innovative Pixels Art

For Jason, the visual approach to presenting a journal narrative supports critical analysis and allows for the inclusion of wider social and cultural concepts, whereby the story is filtered through the work of an artist (see Figure 6.2). What stands out here, in addition to the high-quality artistic work, is the careful application of detailed analytical processes. The particular focus on the market scene in Figure 6.2 captures an aesthetic sense of the original experience. Photographs, recordings and journal entries with reflection were used to produce this image. The use of the Monkey Run logo on the computer screen acknowledged the company for providing the unique experience and was a detail that can lead the reader on to find out more about the organisation. In the end, the comic is not only a way for Jason to present his fieldwork journal and data to a broader audience; it also provides a creative and insightful tool for analysing the data and for encouraging further evaluation and discussion.

Fictionalised accounts

Fictionalisation of research data and fictionalisation as part of research approaches within narrative inquiry, for example, have become more commonly used over the recent past. The reason for the surge in fictionalisation lies with its many advantages. First, fictionalisation enables researchers to meet the ethical requirements of confidentiality and anonymity (Caine et al, 2017). With increased interest in and popularity of person-centred approaches in research, biography, autobiography, life history and anecdotes were suddenly foregrounded (MacLure, 1993). This new focal point raised ethical concerns relating to issues of doing no harm and protecting the identities of research participants. Fictionalisation of accounts became one natural answer within this development. Second, through fictionalisation we can immerse ourselves in the experiential worlds of the other by playfully and creatively considering different perspectives and angles (Hannula, 2003). Fictionalisation therefore enables us to focus on elements of a life story or narrative that may otherwise remain untold. In practice, scholars may draw on an alter ego or a conglomerate, narrative ego to develop and tell the story of the other (LeGuin, 1981). Instead of using a first-person approach or autobiographical 'I', writers employ a third-person narrative. Much like the narrative voice in fiction cannot be equated with the authorial 'I', so it becomes impossible to consider the alter ego as the author-researcher. Consequently, this form of fictionalisation and expanding on experiences protects our own selves as researchers. At the same time, this process of making the familiar strange adds to understanding. Through turning from a first-person to a third-person narrative we can distance ourselves from our own experiences and gain an unusual viewpoint, from which new analytical insights may be gleaned. Third, fictionalisation enables us to explore themes and topics as an additional analytical layer (Caine et al, 2017). Through collating, selecting, assembling and reassembling individual narratives to build merged, conglomerate stories we make sense of and share experiences. In this form of fictionalisation, the author-researcher draws on records from journal entries as well as personal, professional experience and imagination.

Particularly prominent examples of fictionalisation are published within the *Social Fictions Series* by Brill Sense Publishers. The books in this series explore and support the teaching of sociological themes, but are also advertised as stand-alone reading for pleasure. Authors provide an introduction to their fictionalisations, but do not provide an analytical, interpretative commentary. And while they do draw on artistic forms of expression, such as literary devices, they attend to closeness to and clarity of data rather than allowing form and aesthetics take priority. In her novel *October Birds* Jessica Smartt Gullion (2014) draws on her professional experience in sociological research, public health practice and emergency management to explore life in a fictionalised town in Texas at the time of an outbreak of an avian flu pandemic. By contrast, the three novels of Patricia Leavy's *Candy Floss Collection* (2020a) are written as a more light-hearted, humorous installation art of young adults' search for love, friendship and relationships against the backdrop of contemporary New York and Los Angeles, but with a strong link to 1980s' pop culture. The breadth and depth of the series catalogue is fascinating and well worth exploring (see https://brill.com/view/serial/SOCI?contents=toc-38539).

Unfortunately, there are no step-by-step textbooks or how-to handbooks to guide novice author-researchers through the process of developing fictionalised accounts. Indeed, it is one of the biggest criticisms of writing in academic contexts that everyone is expected to learn how to write through osmosis (Jensen, 2017). This book would not be complete if I did not at least offer a starting point for how to develop fictionalisation. If you are interested in developing this aspect of your journalling in greater detail, I recommend consulting books about writing and the writing life. I particularly enjoyed reading *On Writing: A Memoir of the Craft* (King, 2000), *Bird by Bird: Instructions on Writing and Life* (Lamott, 2020), *Fantastic Mr Dahl* (Rosen, 2012) and more recently, *Dæmon Voices: On Stories and Storytelling* (Pullman, 2021).

To demonstrate my way of working and how I tackle fictionalisation in my own practice as author-researcher I draw on some development sheets from my most recent work (Figures 6.3 and 6.4). 'Just One More Time' is a narrative built around the experiences of the COVID-19 pandemic in the UK in the spring of 2020 (Brown, 2021: forthcoming).

I usually begin with identifying an idea or theme that I want to develop before sifting through my journal entries to identify what may be pertinent. I then gather the relevant extracts from all my journals in all their forms and formats – handwritten, computer-typed, artistic creations, neat and messy – and familiarise myself through reading and rereading. This initial reacquainting myself with my own journalling allows me to formulate the key message or messages I intend to convey. In the case of 'Just One More Time', having lived through the pandemic supporting colleagues and students while also dealing with family matters for several months, I wanted to fictionalise my journal entries and make my experiences shareable. Journalling had initially helped me deal with the everyday shock, but revisiting my journal entries was a way to take stock, make an inventory and make sense. The themes I wanted to explore related to the diverging opinions regarding social distancing and to the different levels of empathy displayed even within the social nucleus of a family. My aim was to show the paradox of how the pandemic was simultaneously bringing people together and pushing them apart.

What happens next in the writing process is more difficult to describe, as I create characters with storylines around my key messages. The closest to explaining it is this: I approach the story creation like preparing for teaching with a particular learning objective in mind. In the fictionalisation, my key messages are my learning objectives that I need to communicate. In this case, the starting point for the characters was developing a family where two adults take opposing views regarding social distancing rules. To make the contradictions realistic, but manageable, I decided that the adults would be parents with two children. My next thought process related to the idea of coming together and being pushed apart. I introduced dad's second wife, who would become closer to mum, while drifting apart from dad. As I needed a reason for the push–pull development, I built a backstory for the second wife as being from Italy, homesick and worried about her Italian family. To reinforce the push–pull dynamic, I made dad more relaxed about adhering to distancing rules, while the two wives would be in agreement about complying with the strict guidelines: the mum because she works as a nurse and is shellshocked, and the second wife because she is equally shellshocked from what is happening in her home country and being unable to get there.

Once such basics are fleshed out (Figure 6.3), I approach the development of the actual storyline and how the characters get to interact with one another. For this story, I wanted to capture the reality of the pandemic events like the regular press briefings, school closures

Figure 6.3: Nicole Brown's COVID-19 fiction development

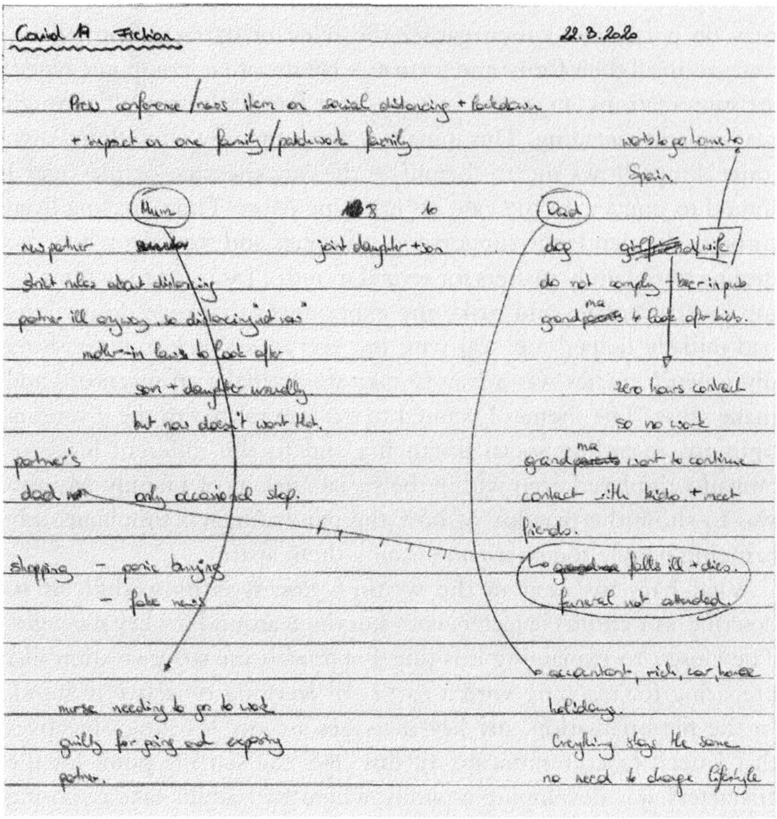

or the closure and reopening of restaurants and bars. I therefore decided that the story needed to be told in scenes.

Once I complete such initial thought processes, character sketches and storylines, I return to my journal entries and using those, I write and rewrite, revise and revisit. At this stage, there is no order or logic, no particular process. Neil Gaiman, the English author of renowned and popular graphic novels and films such as *Stardust*, *Coraline* and *American Gods*, advises us to:

> write down everything that happens in the story, and then in your second draft make it look like you knew what you were doing all along. (Gaiman, 2018)

It is difficult to say how often I really rewrite a story, as I may sometimes only change little details, whereas at other times I prune

Figure 6.4: Nicole Brown's COVID-19 fiction scenes

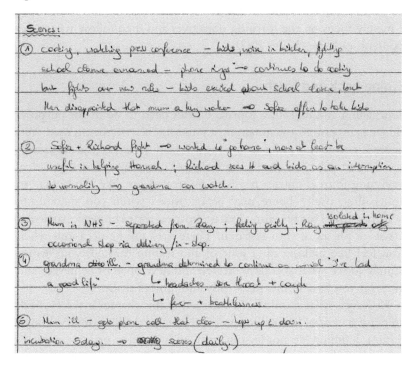

more rigorously. The final version of the COVID-19 story consists of seven, not five, scenes over the period of five months, not one week. More importantly, the final version does not include the characters of the grandma and mum's partner Ray, but instead delves more deeply into the inner lives of the main characters. Much of the characters' interior monologues or emotional turmoil in the final version are lifted from my own journal entries, either directly and fully or as a slightly amended text. This brings me back to the beginning of this section: while I am not comfortable sharing my raw, authentic journalling because I would make myself and others vulnerable, the fictionalisation has helped me distance myself from that vulnerability.

Making sense and sharing through making

Although I have described the process of making and sharing details from research journals through fictionalisation, thus writing, I actually apply the exact same process in different media (Brown, 2019b, c). In those cases, I use journal entries to help me identify key messages that I will then convey through installations or assemblages, instead of creating characters and storylines. I do not have a specific reason or justification for which medium or form of communication I use; I merely focus on the learning objectives and then follow where the content leads me (King, 2000).

Going back and forth

Journalling and revisiting journal entries need to be fit for purpose. There is no point in maintaining a journal if it is not being used. Yet, there is equally no point in forcing yourself to revisit journal entries for no particular reason. In the reality of everyday research practice, revisiting journal entries needs to be treated just like the 'when' of journalling itself. There may be occasions when you specifically schedule times for revisiting journal entries, for example at particular stages or phases of your research. There may also be occasions when you feel like picking up a journal and leafing through your work, simply to see what you have created and developed or achieved, and how far you have come, personally and professionally.

However, what should have emerged in this chapter is the cyclical, iterative nature of journalling and revisiting journal entries. Although I most definitely do not lay out rules on how often or how regularly you must journal or return to entries, I will say this: you need to engage with journalling and your entries in order to make the most of your research journal, and that includes revisiting entries. The different examples from this chapter show that revisiting can mean annotating and analysing previous journal entries, but can also mean reconsidering the entries in different forms and media. In most instances, this reconsideration will lead to a deeper level of understanding, new analytical focal points and anchors, which, in turn, enhance the research process and research life more generally. The key to effectivity, regarding what you do with the research journal, lies in non-judgemental experimentation.

TRY THIS!

Code your entry

Choose an entry from your journal from a longer time ago. To start, you may consciously decide on reading notes or observation notes, thus elements from your journal that are not too emotionally loaded for you. Analyse this journal entry using your chosen framework for coding and analysis. Reflect on the outcome and what you may have gleaned from that exercise. In a second attempt, choose an entry that is more personal and relates to your emotions and experiences, thoughts and reflections. Consider what coding and analysis feel like in this instance. For the third iteration of this coding exercise, I recommend you deliberately choose visual materials from your journal and subject these to coding and analyses. Again, think about what the process feels like and what you may have learned about your materials, but also about yourself and others.

Vent and rant about journalling

The next time you are stuck with your writing or you do not feel like journalling or revisiting your journal entries, use your journal to vent and rant. Experiment with different forms of expression – maybe rip up some scrap pieces of paper, write an entry, make scribbles, draw. The purpose of this exercise is not to create an entry that you will use later, although there is no rule against this. The purpose is to learn to use the scope of journalling as a dumping ground for your emotions. Once you have journalled for a maximum of 15 minutes, stop and take stock. Consider what it feels like to have journalled in this way, and whether or not the process has helped alleviate some of the feeling of being stuck. Make a note – physically or mentally – on what works for you, so that you can repeat as and when needed.

Identify materials to share

Revisit some of your older entries relating to personal thoughts, reflections, emotions or experiences, and identify two or three entries you may be happy to share. Do not worry – you will not be asked to share. This exercise is meant to facilitate the process of getting into the right frame of mind to develop shareable materials from personal entries. Once you have chosen your two or three entries, experiment with different scenarios and forms of communication. Imagine you need to share these entries with other academics as part of sharing best practice or with the wider public as part of a public engagement event or with stakeholders in the context of activist work. Consider the purpose of the dissemination and the audience, and then decide on how you will share your entries. You may decide to create an installation or poetry, a song or painting, stitching or knitting, a fictionalised account or graphic novel. Note that when you use the written form, you may want to change perspectives or narrative voices. Experiment with a range of forms of expression, and then reflect on your learning from the exercise.

7

Considerations of research journalling

Chapter aims

- To demonstrate how research journalling is a valid research activity.

- To consider ethical issues and where to find support for solving ethical matters.

- To present research journalling as a teaching tool.

Introduction

Journalling, like any kind of sense-making, does not happen in a vacuum, but is shaped by our context and circumstances. For example, the choices we make regarding the materials we use for journalling may be dictated by the disciplinary conventions within which we find ourselves. Similarly, whether we follow the principles of visual narratives or of the written form will depend on our own cultural traditions and educational upbringing. Equally, our interpretation of what we can or should do ethically, and how we deal with potentially contentious situations, is governed by institutional directives as well as our personal moral and ethical compasses. Although I have drawn on or hinted at some philosophical, theoretical, ethical and/or pragmatic considerations throughout, Chapters 2 to 6 foreground the practical ideas and strategies for journalling and making the most of a research journal. In no way am I claiming that this book can provide a detailed insight into all considerations. Yet so far, I have introduced ways of working and prompts for journalling and making the most of research journals with what must appear like a reckless disregard for the wider issues of journalling and record-keeping. This chapter remedies that shortcoming, as this book would not be complete if I did not address some of these concerns.

Depending on disciplinary interpretations, personal understanding and scholarly conventions, boundaries become blurred between what constitutes philosophy or theory and theoretical frameworks or methodology, for example. Ethics may be described as part of and integral to methodology as well as a philosophical outlook and a foundation to research life, and life more generally (Kara, 2018). Therefore, I consciously foreground and reconnect here the tentative threads from previous chapters in broader themes rather than narrow categories. By doing so, I hope to provide food for thought regarding the process of journalling, while expanding on what has gone before and offering new threads, threads that are beyond the scope of this book, but that you may wish to pursue to make even more of your research journal.

Theoretical frameworks and the research journal

Throughout the book I have cautiously provided examples for how theoretical frameworks relate to the practice of journalling. After all, there is a long tradition of keeping research journals, especially within the context of professional development and learning (Stevens and Cooper, 2009). Where I talked about revisiting journal entries, I outlined how theoretical frameworks may shape the way you approach that reconsideration. Within the context of reflexivity, I mentioned the role of research journals as a tool to help identify which theoretical frameworks or philosophical outlooks may underpin your own thoughts. In this sense, the research journal is not linked to a particular school of thought we buy into. It is incredibly adaptable and it allows us to apply different methods and lenses. As a result, unfortunately, journalling may be interpreted as an unscholarly, unacademic and atheoretical endeavour.

This misconception is further compounded by the fact that some entries are indeed very personal and so cannot and will not ever be shared. The issue at play here is not unique to research journalling, but affects particular kinds of research more generally. Practice As Research and Practice-Led Inquiry (Smith and Dean, 2009; Barrett and Bolt, 2010; Nelson, 2013), material methods (Woodward, 2019) and Embodied Inquiry (Leigh and Brown, 2021) all suffer that same fate of being criticised for being atheoretical and unscholarly. However, this criticism could not be further from the truth. Rather than subscribing to one theoretical framework, you engage with many. This means that you need to build quite an arsenal of tools and wide foundational knowledge to be able to draw on what is most suitable.

For some, this pragmatic eclecticism comes naturally; for others this pick-and-mix approach belongs to the sweets section in a supermarket, but not to the fields of academic research. The fact is that in using journalling systematically as a basis for analysis and dissemination, we open ourselves to this criticism.

Established academics will find it easier to deal with the consequences and potential fall-out of engaging with the seemingly atheoretical activity that is research journalling, not because they have a better way of defending the quality, validity and robustness of their entries. Established scholars will find it easier because they already have a career trajectory and an academic profile, whereas early career researchers still need to develop these while experiencing the pressures of fixed-term contracts and/or general job insecurity. This does not mean that you should shy away from research journalling. It merely means that you need to be prepared to counter potential criticisms.

So here is what happens in reality in the process of research journalling: instead of putting theoretical frameworks first, you link theory, methods and practice in an iterative spiral that takes you deeper into that interconnected space of theory, methods and practice. As you delve into that space, you introduce new or different theoretical frameworks and philosophical outlooks into the journalling practice, thereby potentially breaking down long-held disciplinary boundaries. Yet, through that engagement, you define your beliefs, deepen your understanding and justify your choices. Eclecticism regarding theoretical choices, therefore, does not mean to be ignorant of theories, nor does it mean to employ a catch-all terminology to cover up the lack of a theoretical framework. Instead, being eclectic is a conscious choice to find the most suitable approach for the task at hand.

A space to play: theorisation and the research journal

Bearing in mind my argument that research journalling is not an atheoretical, unscholarly activity, it is time to reassess what the research journal truly is. I have presented the research journal as a space to play, an opportunity to experiment and as a working document. Ultimately, it comes down again to purpose and aim. The sections in our research journal that consist of trackers are indeed only working documents to make our lives more manageable and to relieve us from the worries of missing deadlines. Yet, the parts of our research journal where we revisit journal entries are more than just management tools or organisational strategies. Entries can, of course, be revisited for entertainment value only. I remember a particularly enjoyable afternoon spent with my mum, when we reread the journal entries from my youth about my horse riding 'adventures'. My journalling had been all about the horses, their behaviours and their characteristics. I had stylised myself as 'The Horse Whisperer', when, in fact, I had genuinely been scared of the animals.

In most instances, however, revisiting the journal entries affords us to engage scholarly and intellectually. This engagement may feel playful, especially when we experiment with new approaches of analysis or methods of communication. In short, journalling is

> a process of continuous discovery, filled with correspondences and contradictions, intuition and surprise, serendipity and discipline. (Stewart, 2010: 124)

Engaging in such a playful way does not mean the engagement is not academic. What I am proposing here is that the research journal is a space to experiment with theoretical, and indeed conceptual, frameworks. You can revisit your journal entries by applying particular lenses. If you usually draw on functionalist theory, you may want to 'play' with feminist theory. If you tend to apply co-construction and constructivism, you may want to 'play' with objectivism or behaviourism. Similarly, you may 'play' with different modes of communication and forms of expression to develop theoretical and conceptual understanding. If you usually tend to write, you may want to paint, or if you routinely sketch and knit, you may want to engage with soundscapes or music. You do not need to compose, but merely collate a relevant song list. As I mentioned earlier, this initial 'playing' will help you identify your innermost beliefs, which, in turn, facilitates the development of an authentic researcher self. Once you have gone through that stage, you will be able to develop good quality, solid validity and robustness in and with your journal entries.

We can learn here from Practice As Research, where the interconnection between practice and theory, thus the doing and the thinking about doing, is the foundational basis for and of research. The 'practical doing-thinking' and the 'more abstract conceptual thinking' (Nelson, 2013: 29) are two facets of the same coin that cannot exist without each other, as 'theory emerges from a reflexive practice, at the same time as practice is informed by theory' (Barrett, 2010: 29). Simplified, a practitioner does and reflects on the doing to arrive at a theorisation, while the theorisation feeds back into the creative practice. My argument is that in these theoretical deliberations we can interpret the conceptualisation of research journalling as a form of practice, so that Practice As Research becomes Journalling As Research. As research journallers we journal and reflect on the journalling to arrive at a theorisation, while, simultaneously, that theorisation seeps back into our journalling practices. The research journal is therefore an opportunity to academicise what may otherwise appear trivial or mundane. Research journalling is research.

Broaden your horizon

As the foundational principle of research journalling is eclecticism, we journallers need to learn of and about a wide range of frameworks. We cannot claim to be eclectic if our knowledge of theories is so limited that we only have one or two at our disposal. Instead, we need to be open towards and seek out new kinds of knowledge. Disciplinary, inter- and trans-disciplinary traditions are a great starting point to identify relevant theories in cognate subjects. Our search for the new, the different or the marginalised should not stop there.

In the UK context of higher education, and indeed globally, we are orienting ourselves strongly by the standards of Euro-Western Anglo-centric conventions and traditions with a rather unhealthy disregard for other forms of knowledge and truth. If we want to make the most of our journals and further enhance our journalling practices, we should look to those systems that are unknown and unusual to us. Please note: I am not saying that we should appropriate those knowledge systems and traditions; I am saying that we should humbly look to those knowledge systems and traditions with the respect they deserve, to learn from them.

For example, across most European and Western countries, we understand the human sensorium to consist of the five senses – sight, sound, smell, taste and touch. When we therefore talk about 'training our senses', as I proposed in the exercise in Chapter 3, we focus on sight, sound, smell, taste and touch. However, what if the conceptualisation of the five senses as advocated by Karl Marx (1932), and further developed by a number of esteemed philosophers, historians and anthropologists, is inaccurate or just plain wrong? Indeed, research from within the disciplinary scopes and on the cusp of anatomy, biology, physiology, philosophy, psychology and embodiment outlines a range of interpretative systems and categories that deconstruct the idea of five senses in humans. Our sensory system is much broader than the limitation of the five categories suggests. Our sensorium includes balance and movement, pressure (the experience of strength and weakness or flexibility and stiffness), breathing, fatigue, pain, itch, temperature, appetite and expulsion from the body (the experiences of sneezes, coughs, hiccups, vomiting and the like) (Eccleston, 2016). Already we can see how the 'Train your senses' exercise in Chapter 3 would provide new sets of information and insights, if we were to include our observations on movement, balance, breathing, fatigue or temperature. The issue goes further. How we are brought up sensorily has a bearing on our use of language and our understanding of the world. In a fascinating TED Talk, the cognitive scientist Lera Boroditsky draws on her research to explain how experiences, language and understanding intersect (2018). Boroditsky highlights how sensory experiences are reflected in and shaped by language, which, in turn, has an impact on how the world is viewed and understood:

> Unlike English, the Kuuk Thaayorre language spoken in Pormpuraaw [Aboriginal community in northern Australia] does not use relative spatial terms such as left and right. Rather Kuuk Thaayorre speakers talk in terms of absolute cardinal directions (north, south, east, west, and so forth). Of course, in English we also use cardinal direction terms but only for large spatial scales. We would not say, for example, "They set the salad forks southeast of the dinner forks – the philistines!" But in Kuuk Thaayorre cardinal directions are used at all scales. This means one ends up saying things like "the cup is southeast of the plate" or "the boy standing to the south of Mary is my brother". (Boroditsky, 2011: 64)

As a consequence of this particular understanding and expression of space, temporality is communicated differently. Where English speakers organise temporal events from left to right, and Hebrew speakers from right to left, thus in the direction of how we read, Kuuk Thaayorre speakers express temporality from east to west (Boroditsky, 2011).

These differences have a bearing on how we view our own bodies and beings within the context of our worlds and experiences (Hockey and Allen-Collinson, 2009), which, in turn, impacts our views of and on positionality and reflexivity. If we are not aware of a sense of balance, we will not take note of that sense during our research endeavours, and so will not record any relevant information in the research journal. Instead of organising and sorting from left to right, the direction of how we read, perhaps we should try to use a right to left or bottom to top arrangement.

Similarly, we ought to reengage with our heritage of traditional knowledge. 'Traditional knowledge' is an umbrella term for the information, skills and knowledge handed down from generation to generation. This kind of knowledge is often applied implicitly, tacitly and subconsciously, but makes up, or at least contributes to, our cultural identity. Commonly, traditional knowledge and traditional knowledge systems are 'oral, unsystematised, undocumented and under imminent danger of getting irretrievably lost' (Jha, 2009: 10). Yet, the embedded and embodied traditional knowledge spans disciplinary boundaries of medicine, agriculture, production, construction, the sciences, the arts, architecture, mathematics, astronomy, astrology, religion, crafts and trades (Jha, 2009). Of course, it is impossible to learn or apply all intricate details of all cultures and societies, but we should be aware of the wealth of knowledge that is out there for us to tap into. We could learn from our parents and grandparents how to sew or knit, or we could have our aunts and uncles show us how to carve wood and bake bread, or forage for edibles. The opportunities are endless. Developing these traditional and new skills and knowledge will expand our horizons so we can build on that in our journalling. But as the theory will inform the practice, so can the practice of learning these skills inform the process of journalling and making sense. Let us therefore respectfully experiment with and learn from all knowledge.

Whose story, whose voice? The ethics of a research journal

The ethics of the research journal is probably the biggest concern when journalling. I have mentioned ethics briefly in Chapters 4 and 6, and then hinted again at ethical considerations in earlier sections of this chapter. Although ethical behaviours, academic and ethical misconduct are now considered in greater detail than ever before, the universalist understanding of ethics, the one-size-fits-all approach, is still predominant (Kara, 2018). This is despite calls for the consideration of ethics as ongoing processes for the entirety of the research (Ramcharan and Cutcliffe, 2001; Cutcliffe and Ramcharan, 2002; Kelley et al, 2013). But where do the research journal and the act of journalling fit here? As the research journal is hardly ever discussed, it does not usually feature in ethical considerations or applications for ethical approvals. Theoretically, therefore, there is no guidance and, more importantly, no limitation regarding what we do with our research journals or how we deal with research entries. In practice, we should not be led by the guidelines and requirements of ethics committees, but strive to be ethical journallers.

Journal entries are private and personal affairs, but in our journalling as a sense-making activity we are bound to tell stories or anecdotes that include or refer to other people. In reality, as soon as we save conversations and commentaries, we include other people's stories and voices, usually without their knowledge. Ethically, this is questionable. Worse still, in Chapter 4, I actively advised the mining and siphoning off of blog posts, commentaries, social media posts or chat texts from WhatsApp or other messenging applications as a form of journalling. Again, this is incredibly problematic because others do not know and have no control over how their content is used. Yet, I also talked about keeping good records so we can provide evidence regarding data as well as in relation to matters of academic integrity or misconduct. Clearly, when journalling there is a tension between including and leaving out others' stories and content.

Resolving this matter is no easy feat, especially as research journals are not commonly considered in ethics guidance or approval processes. To find coherent, meaningful ways of identifying and dealing with ethical issues, let us return to the notion that research journalling is research. Thinking about what is being recorded, how journal entries are revisited and treated, research journalling is ethnographic and autoethnographic in nature. Put simply, ethnography is the study (-graphy) of culture (ethno-), whereas autoethnography is the study (-graphy) of self (auto-) as related to or an example of culture (-ethno-) (Chang, 2016). I am not asking that as journallers we fully subscribe to ethnographic or autoethnographic traditions or conventions. After all, as has been described earlier, research journalling is not linked to one specific theoretical framework or approach, but is open to many. I do, however, suggest that some of the tensions we encounter in research journalling are not too dissimilar from the issues that ethnographers and autoethnographers must navigate as part of their research. We can therefore look to and learn from ethnographic or autoethnographic ethics processes.

(Auto)ethnography needs to account for procedural ethics, situational ethics or ethics in practice as well as relational ethics (Guillemin and Gillam, 2004; Lapadat, 2017). Procedural ethics concerns informed consent, privacy, confidentiality and protection from harm. Situational ethics or ethics in practice refers to what researchers do in response to what happens in the field; for example, if a person discloses discomfort or reveals they are at risk in some way. Relational ethics refers to the relations and relationships that are built in the field, and which the (auto)ethnographer tends to through dignity, respect and mutual, interdependent values. In short, where (auto)ethnographers record, select, assemble, analyse and reassemble data, they do so with the obligation to consider relations as well as the responsibility these relations are linked with (Roth, 2009).

In particular, (auto)ethnographers recognise and debate becoming voyeurs (Tamas, 2009), and taking control of a narrative that may not necessarily be theirs (Dauphinee, 2010). In research journalling, we also consider others and our selves in relation to others as we journal. We may not do so in the same systematic way (auto)ethnographers do, but the initial considerations are the same. We need to find the right balance between telling *our* experiences and considering those of others. Through the process of our own journalling, we may misrepresent or hurt others, and change the dynamics of our relationship with them (Ellis, 2007). At the same time, journalling and reporting covertly is also problematic, even if it may be the preferred approach in some contexts (Herrera, 1999; Calvey, 2018).

The controversies surrounding ethics of care as well as the responsibility for and ownership of a narrative are best exemplified in the responses to *On The Run: Fugitive Life in an American City* (Goffman, 2015). For her research, Alice Goffman, a white, female, university student, immersed herself in the culture of a disadvantaged, predominantly Black neighbourhood in Philadelphia. In her book, she reports on criminal activities, police surveillance and gang behaviours she had observed and had been involved with to some extent. Although initially the book was highly praised and well received, subsequent investigations and explorations uncovered inaccuracies, discrepancies and embellishments, which, in turn, led to questions of ethics: is it morally or ethically right for a white advantaged student to enter the difficult, impoverished, disadvantaged Black lives, when she has the privilege to move out of the field and others do not? Is it acceptable to observe and participate in criminal activities without reporting them? The methodological note in the book's appendix highlights further issues around the welfare and wellbeing of the researcher herself.

With that in mind, we need to ask ourselves how we can make our journalling ethical. Carolyn Ellis (2007) instructs us to take into account the greater good of research, to be ethical (auto)ethnographers, to not censure our initial writing, and to inform others and seek their consent when we write about them. Yet, she also shows us that sometimes these choices are not straightforward and that we may have our reasons to not follow this advice. In those instances, we need to be able to justify our choices and explain our reasoning. Ultimately,

I believe that most people want to do the right thing, the sensible thing. As human beings, we long to live meaningful lives that seek the good. As friends, we long to have trusting relationships that care for others. As researchers, we long to do ethical research that makes a difference. To come close to these goals, we constantly have to consider which questions to ask, which secrets to keep, and which truths are worth telling. (Ellis, 2007: 26)

Pedagogy and the research journal

Where I have discussed the practicalities of research journalling throughout this book, I have emphasised relevance and advantages in relation to research development, as well as regarding professional and personal growth. Research journalling is research, but in addition, the journal organises us and manages our time, offers us a respite from everyday tasks and represents a dumping ground for our emotional baggage. What I have not elaborated on so far is that the research journal may also function as a teaching tool. Journalling is often used to help students achieve particular learning objectives (Boud, 2001; Moon, 2006) through applying learning content (Hampton and Morrow, 2003; Thorpe, 2004). Journalling is also incorporated into teaching as an opportunity for students to practise critical thinking and academic writing skills (Kerka, 2002; Watson, 2010). Not only should we recognise these additional benefits of journals; we ought to take advantage of them in the process of our own research journalling.

Researcher voice and identity

Within the scope of ethical considerations relating to research journalling we briefly reflected on voice in the context of ownership of a story and taking responsibility for representation. However, voice and identity also need to be examined from the journaller's point of view. Research into lived experiences informs us about identity formation among doctoral students (Hall and Burns, 2009; Foot et al, 2014; Sala-Bubaré and Castelló, 2017) as well as about the role writing plays as an emotional process of sense-making (Cotterall, 2013; Aitchison and Mowbray, 2013). Research journalling therefore is an extension of and complement to that process.

Developing an authorial voice or researcher identity is difficult due to the tacit, implicit, undocumented and unarticulated knowledge that needs to be acquired. The issue is more complex, though. Often, we do not know how we have arrived at a particular point, and so we literally cannot articulate the process. Let me use my own career trajectory as an example. I started my professional life as a secondary school teacher, and I worked as a translator, teacher-educator and lecturer in education, and for some of that time I was also a doctoral student. Consequently, I have defined and redefined my professional identity in several iterations. There were some milestones for changes, but in most instances the shift was gradual and unnoticeable until the transition had been completed. If I was asked now, I would describe myself as a social science researcher and practitioner. Yet it evades me when and how I have 'become' that.

It is not my intention here to present details of critical language awareness and critical literacy pedagogies that provide the basis for debates around writing the self into research and developing identity through language (see Viete and Ha, 2007; Jackson and Mazzei, 2008). I do wish to mention, however, that through the practice of journalling, in written or other forms, we investigate and reflect on our selves, thus we explore our own voice and identity, consciously or subconsciously:

> In academic writing, authors develop a recognizable and individual sameness with respect to their body of work, which contributes to inferences regarding their voices. They become associated with particular kinds of texts, particular topics, and citations of particular others, and cues to their identity come through those commonalities as well as the language that they use. (Nelson and Castelló, 2012: 51)

We can write and revise or work and rework our documents, and we can incorporate feedback into each edit. But ultimately, the development of authorial voice and research identity is implicit, tacit, by stealth, until eventually that shift happens that turns us from student to expert authorities in our field (Morton and Storch, 2019). Where attempts are made to articulate guidance to facilitate this learning process, there is a risk of oversimplification and misrepresentation in categorical, but contentious, statements such as 'do not use the first person', 'do not use the passive voice', 'write scholarly' or 'do not use jargon'. As research journalling allows us to experiment with theories, so we may want to 'play' with language, perspective, voice and identity.

Teaching research journalling

While experimenting to find an authorial voice or researcher identity is difficult, facilitating that process and supporting others in their development is practically impossible. This takes us back to the initial discussions around reflection, and how reflective practice is notoriously difficult to teach (Rogers, 2001). Teaching reflective practice is like taking a horse to water: you can take it to the water, but you cannot make it drink. The same applies to teaching authorial voice, supporting others to improve their writing skills and, ultimately, to research journalling. It is possible to provide guidance and support around the principles of reflective practice, and it is also possible to offer templates to facilitate the process. Yet, it is impossible to make others engage.

I cannot make you engage in research journalling. I can only 'provide sparks for existing fires by offering useful techniques, tips, and insights' (Ludwig, 2011b: 9). You need to bring the relevant interest, familiarity with basic principles and the right frame of mind. I am not sure if a 'journalling mindset' is a thing, but I know that attitudinal dispositions do play a role. You may want to consider *Mindset: Changing the Way You Think to Fulfil Your Potential* (Dweck, 2017), *Black Box Thinking: The Surprising Truth About Success* (Syed, 2015) or *Grit: Why Passion and Resilience are the Secrets to Success* (Duckworth, 2017) as examples for relevant characteristics and attitudes. To achieve success, the authors of these books recommend being passionate, accepting failure as opportunities for growth, and to not give up. The exact same advice is offered in publications about journalling (Ludwig, 2011a, b; Miller, 2017), in relation to writing in academia (Jensen, 2017) as well as about art and creative work (Brereton, 2009; Hobbs, 2014; Laporte, 2017). The definition of what constitutes success matters. Success in relation to research journalling is not producing aesthetically accomplished and pleasing journal entries. Success in research journalling is purposefully picking up the research journal, using appropriate tools, creating relevant entries and meaningfully revisiting previous work. Success is journalling.

8

Conclusion

Journalling is not new, and the value of journalling is undisputed. There have never been more different categories of journals: learning journals; diaries; dream books or logs; autobiographies, life stories or memoirs; spiritual journals; professional journals; interactive reading logs; theory logs; and electronic journals (Hiemstra, 2011). And these nine types are before the notebooks, sketchbooks, art journals, ideas boxes, experiment logs and all the individual trackers associated with bullet journalling.

This book has shown that journalling means having a working document for your personal purposes, whatever they may be. We know that research journalling can be experienced as a difficult task, especially as it is associated with particular expectations of what journals and entries look like. Academic communities are often not helpful because many of us have developed our own personal practices over the years, without actively engaging in why particular ways of recording and writing work for us and why others do not. Also, what works for me may not necessarily work for others, and it may not work for you. The reality of journalling is best exemplified with an image from Aine McAllister, whose poetic inquiry journal entry was presented in Chapter 4. In addition to keeping a conventional journal in book form, Aine also often uses post-it notes, as a form of agile management. Journalling therefore is not always straightforward, but may make the journalling process look messy. What has not entered the conversation so far, however, is that in addition to her scholarly and poetic work, Aine is also mum to a cute toddler, and often works with her little boy Áedán on her lap, who will then also 'work' (see Figure 8.1).

I have included Aine's image in this Conclusion to reinforce what I set out to do with this book: to show that research journalling comes in many forms. The point of a research journal is not to entertain a particular notion of the research journal. The point is to journal sensibly, effectively and meaningfully to fit the purposes of the research work we undertake and that suits our lifestyle and personality. With that, let me revisit three key messages of this book.

Figure 8.1: Aine McAllister's journalling as a working mum

The key messages

1. Anything and everything goes

Of course, we need to be ethical in our work, but we also need to approach research journalling free from rules or expectations. You may well aim for a neat, organised and pretty research journal, but if this is a standard that is too difficult to maintain, then aim for something else. At the end of the day, you want the research journal to work for you.

2. Journalling must be fit for purpose

Sometimes a journal entry only consists of bullet points; at other times you may create an elaborate short story cycle. Both entries are valid and relevant; they just have different purposes. As you need to eradicate the idea that a research journal has a particular look, you need to eliminate the notion that a journal entry has a particular look. Through experimenting with form and formats, it is more likely that we will continue maintaining our research journal, as it naturally slots into our busy schedule and better fits our modern lifestyle.

3. Journalling requires a specific attitude

Purposeful journalling on its own is not sufficient. We need to be open to the new, trust our own instincts, tap into our playfulness and creativity and, most importantly, expect the process of journalling to be fun. Of course, I am under no illusion. Approaching journalling with the expectation of fun does not necessarily make it fun. Yet, I write from personal experience when I say that journalling without the pressures of meeting conventions is not a chore, and actually is fun most of the time.

Throughout this book, I demonstrate that in order to make the most of a research journal we need to demystify it. To this end, I provide ideas, strategies, techniques and food for thought, not to lecture or teach, but to inspire and ignite your imagination. I acknowledge that in academic circles the process of research journalling is hardly ever discussed, but I also outline how the value of research journalling can be theorised, explained and justified. What has perhaps remained implicit so far is the immense value research journalling can bring. As Susan Sontag states about journalling, it is:

> superficial to understand the journal as just a receptacle for one's private, secret thoughts – like a confidante who is deaf, dumb, and illiterate. In the journal I do not just express myself more openly than I could do to any person; I create myself.
>
> The journal is a vehicle for my sense of selfhood. It represents me as emotionally and spiritually independent. Therefore (alas) it does not simply record my actual, daily life but rather – in many cases – offers an alternative to it. (Sontag, 2012: 128)

Through experimenting with different forms and media, the process of journalling enables the researcher to enter realms that would otherwise remain hidden. As such, it is not impossible or unusual as a journaller to be surprised by our own scholarly engagement, insightful theorsisations or emotional connections. When we are freed from the expectations of *the* research journal, journalling is an opportunity to enter a conversation with our selves, and to learn about ourselves and others. In turn, we are able to make meaningful connections and draw perceptive conclusions about our data, but also about our own positioning within the research specifically, as well as our disciplinary contexts and the academic community more generally. In short, the research journal offers endless possibilities for our journey, from the inception of an idea through to the dissemination of research findings, for scholarly debate and professional development, as well as for personal growth and wellbeing.

References

Aitchison, C. and Mowbray, S. (2013) 'Doctoral women: Managing emotions, managing doctoral studies', *Teaching in Higher Education*, 18(8), 859–70.

Alvesson, M. and Skoldberg, K. (2000) *Reflexive Methodology: New Vistas for Qualitative Researchers*, London: SAGE Publications Ltd.

Amabile, T.M. and Fisher, C.M. (2009) 'Stimulate Creativity by Fueling Passion', in E.A. Locke (ed) *Handbook of Principles of Organizational Behavior*, Chichester: John Wiley & Sons, 331–41.

Amabile, T.M., Hadley, C.N. and Kramer, S.J. (2002) 'Creativity under the gun', *Harvard Business Review*, 80, 52–63.

Amabile, T.M., Conti, R., Coon, H., Lazenby, J. and Herron, M. (1996) 'Assessing the work environment for creativity', *Academy of Management Journal*, 39(5), 1154–84.

Atkinson, P.A. (2020) *Writing Ethnographically*, London: SAGE Publications Ltd.

Ayobi, A., Sonne, T., Marshall, P. and Cox, A.L. (2018) 'Flexible and Mindful Self-Tracking: Design Implications from Paper Bullet Journals', in *Proceedings of the 2018 CHI Conference on Human Factors in Computing Systems*, 1–14.

Ballenger, B. (2014) *The Curious Researcher: A Guide to Writing Research Papers* (8th edn), London: Pearson.

Barone, T. and Eisner, E.W. (2012) *Arts Based Research*, London: SAGE Publications Ltd.

Barrett, E. (2010) 'The Magic Is in Handling', in E. Barrett and B. Bolt (eds) *Practice as Research: Approaches to Creative Arts Enquiry*, London: Bloomsbury, 27–34.

Barrett, E. and Bolt, B. (eds) (2010) *Practice as Research: Approaches to Creative Arts Enquiry*, London: Bloomsbury.

Bassot, B. (2020) *The Research Journal: A Reflective Tool for Your First Independent Research Project*, Bristol: Policy Press.

Beale, B., Cole, R., Hillege, S., McMaster, R. and Nagy, S. (2004) 'Impact of in-depth interviews on the interviewer: Roller coaster ride', *Nursing and Health Sciences*, 6(2), 141–7.

Beaumont, S.L. (2012) 'Art therapy approaches for identity problems during adolescence', *Canadian Art Therapy Association Journal*, 25(1), 7–14.

Berman, M.G., Jonides, J. and Kaplan, S. (2008) 'The cognitive benefits of interacting with nature', *Psychological Science*, 19(12), 1207–12.

Bjorøy, A., Madigand, S. and Nylund, D. (2016) 'The Practice of Therapeutic Letter Writing in Narrative Therapy', in B. Douglas, E. Kasket, R. Woolfe, S. Strawbridge and V. Galbraith (eds) *The Handbook of Counselling Psychology* (4th edn), London: SAGE Publications Ltd, Chapter 20.

Blommaert, J. (2006) 'Applied ethnopoetics', *Narrative Inquiry*, 16(1), 181–90.

Bolner, M.S., Poirier, G.A., Welsh, T.S. and Pace, E. (2013) *The Research Process: Books and Beyond* (5th edn), Dubuque, IA: Kendall Hunt.

Bonnet, J.L., Cordell, S.A., Cordell, J., Duque, G.J., MacKintosh, P.J. and Peters, A. (2013) 'The apprentice researcher: Using undergraduate researchers' personal essays to shape instruction and services', *Portal: Libraries and the Academy*, 13(1), 37–59.

Boroditsky, L. (2011) 'How language shapes thought', *Scientific American*, 304(2), 62–5.

Boroditsky, L. (2018) 'How language shapes thought' [Video]. YouTube, 2 May. Available at: www.youtube.com/watch?v=RKK7wGAYP6k

Boud, D. (2001) 'Using Journal Writing to Enhance Reflective Practice', in L.M. English and M.A. Gillen (eds) *Promoting Journal Writing in Adult Education*, San Francisco, CA: Jossey-Bass, vol 90, 9–18.

Bradbury-Jones, C., Taylor, J. and Herber, O.R. (2014) 'Vignette development and administration: A framework for protecting research participants', *International Journal of Social Research Methodology*, 17(4), 427–40.

Braun, V. and Clarke, V. (2006) 'Using thematic analysis in psychology', *Qualitative Research in Psychology*, 3(2), 77–101

Braun, V. and Clarke, V. (2019) 'Reflecting on reflexive thematic analysis', *Qualitative Research in Sport, Exercise and Health*, 1–9.

Brereton, R. (2009) *Sketchbooks: The Hidden Art of Designers, Illustrators and Creatives*, London: Laurence King Publishing.

Bretag, T. and Mahmud, S. (2009) 'Self-plagiarism or appropriate textual re-use?', *Journal of Academic Ethics*, 7(3), 193–205.

Bridgewater, P. (2011) 'SMART or CUTE – What makes a good target?', *Botanical Journal of the Linnean Society*, 166(3), 240–9.

Brookfield, S. (1995) *Becoming a Critically Reflective Teacher*, San Francisco, CA: Jossey-Bass.

Brown, N. (2019a) 'Emerging researcher perspectives: Finding your people: My challenge of developing a creative research methods network', *International Journal of Qualitative Methods*, 18, 1–3.

Brown, N. (2019b) '"Listen to your gut": A reflexive approach to data analysis', *The Qualitative Report*, 24(13), 31–43.

Brown, N. (2019c) 'Identity boxes: Using materials and metaphors to elicit experiences', *International Journal of Social Research Methodology*, 22(5), 487–501.

Brown, N. (2020) 'The "I" in Fibromyalgia: The Construction of Academic Identity Under the Influence of Fibromyalgia', unpublished doctoral dissertation, University of Kent, Canterbury.

Brown, N. (2021) *Lived Experiences of Ableism in Academia*, Bristol: Policy Press.

Brown, N. (2021: forthcoming) '"Just One More Time": A Family's Experience of Social Distancing in the Times of the COVID-19 Pandemic', in S. Bruzzi and M. Biriotti (eds) *Lockdown Culture: The Arts, Humanities and Covid-19*, London: UCL Press.

Brown, N. and Leigh, J. (2020) *Ableism in Academia*, London: UCL Press.

Brown, N. and Leigh, J. (2021) *Embodied Inquiry*, London: Bloomsbury.

Brown, N. and Morgan, C. (2021) 'Rhythmanalysis as a Method to Account for Time in Qualitative Research', in B.C. Clift, J. Gore, S. Gustafsson, S. Bekker and I.C. Batlle (eds) *Temporality in Qualitative Inquiry: Theories, Methods, and Practices*, Abingdon: Routledge, 111–26.

Bruno, A. and Dell'Aversana, G. (2017) 'Reflective practice for psychology students: The use of reflective journal feedback in higher education', *Psychology Learning & Teaching*, 16(2), 248–60.

Burgess, R.G. (1981) 'Keeping a research diary', *Cambridge Journal of Education*, 11(1), 75–83.

Butros, A. and Taylor, S. (2010) 'Managing information: Evaluating and selecting citation management software, a look at EndNote, RefWorks, Mendeley and Zotero', in *Netting Knowledge: Two Hemispheres/One World: Proceedings of the 36th IAMSLIC Annual Conference*, IAMSLIC, 17–21.

Buzan, T. and Buzan, B. (2002) *How to Mind Map*, London: Thorsons.

Buzan, T. and Buzan, B. (2006) *The Mind Map Book*, London: Pearson Education.

Caine, V., Murphy, M.S., Estefan, A., Clandinin, D.J., Steeves, P. and Huber, J. (2017) 'Exploring the purposes of fictionalization in narrative inquiry', *Qualitative Inquiry*, 23(3), 215–21.

Calvey, D. (2018) 'Covert: The Fear and Fascination of a Methodological Pariah', in R. Iphofen and M. Tolich (eds) *The SAGE Handbook of Qualitative Research Ethics*, London: SAGE Publications Ltd, 470–85.

Candy, L. (2011) 'Research and Creative Practice', in L. Candy and E.A. Edmonds (eds) *Interacting: Art, Research and the Creative Practitioner*, Faringdon: Libri Publishing, 33–59.

Carroll, R. (2018) *The Bullet Journal Method: Track the Past, Order the Present, Design the Future*, Harmondsworth: Penguin.

Chadwick, R. (2017) 'Embodied methodologies: Challenges, reflections and strategies', *Qualitative Research*, 17(1), 54–74.

Chandler, C.I. and Reynolds, J. (2013) *ACT Consortium Guidance: Qualitative Research Protocol Template with Example Tools and SOPS*, London: London School of Hygiene and Tropical Medicine. Available at: www.actconsortium.org/data/files/resources/72/ Qualitative-Research-Protocol-Template-with-example-Tools-and-SOPs_Dec2013.docx

Chang, H. (2016) *Autoethnography as Method*, Abingdon: Routledge.

Charmaz, K. (2006) *Constructing Grounded Theory: A Practical Guide Through Qualitative Analysis*, London: SAGE Publications Ltd.

Chiseri-Strater, E. (1996) 'Turning in Upon Ourselves: Positionality, Subjectivity, and Reflexivity in Case Study and Ethnographic Research', in P. Mortensen and G.E. Kirsch (eds) *Ethics and Representation in Qualitative Studies of Literacy*, Urbana, IL: NCTE (National Council of Teachers of English), 115–33.

Clarke, R. (2006) 'Plagiarism by academics: More complex than it seems', *Journal of the Association for Information Systems*, 7(2), 91–121.

Clifford, J. (1990) 'Notes on (Field) Notes', in R. Sanjek (ed) *Fieldnotes: The Makings of Anthropology*, Ithaca, NY: Cornell University Press, 47–70.

Costantino, P.M., De Lorenzo, M.N. and Kobrinski, E.J. (2002) *Developing a Professional Teaching Portfolio: A Guide for Success*, Boston, MA: Allyn & Bacon.

Cotterall, S. (2013) 'More than just a brain: Emotions and the doctoral experience', *Higher Education Research & Development*, 32(2), 174–87.

Covey, S.R. (1989) *The 7 Habits of Highly Effective People: An Extraordinary Step-by-step Guide to Achieving the Human Characteristics that Really Create Success*, New York: Simon & Schuster.

Crown Journals (2019) *Scientist's Journal: Daily Research Diary Journal Logbook Guide for Scientists to Log, Write In and Record All Procedures of their Research*, Crown Journals.

Cutcliffe, J.R. and Ramcharan, P. (2002) 'Leveling the playing field? Exploring the merits of the ethics-as-process approach for judging qualitative research proposals', *Qualitative Health Research*, 12(7), 1000–10.

Dabner, D., Stewart, S. and Vickress, A. (2017) *Graphic Design School: The Principles and Practice of Graphic Design*, Chichester: John Wiley & Sons.

D'Cruz, H., Gillingham, P. and Mendelez, S. (2007) 'Reflexivity, its meanings and relevance for social work: A critical review of the literature', *British Journal of Social Work*, 37(1), 73–90.

Dauphinee, E. (2010) 'The ethics of autoethnography', *Review of International Studies*, 36(3), 799–818.

Day, T. and Tosey, P. (2011) 'Beyond SMART? A new framework for goal setting', *Curriculum Journal*, 22(4), 515–34.

Deaver, S.P. and McAuliffe, G. (2009) 'Reflective visual journaling during art therapy and counselling internships: A qualitative study', *Reflective Practice*, 10(5), 615–32.

Decoo, W. (2001) *Crisis on Campus: Confronting Academic Misconduct*, Cambridge, MA: MIT Press.

Delacruz, E. and Bales, S. (2010) 'Creating history, telling stories, and making special: Portfolios, scrapbooks, and sketchbooks', *Art Education*, 63(1), 33–9.

Delamont, S. (2018) 'Truth is Not Linked to Political Virtue: Problems with Positionality', Keynote Presentation at the Fourth Annual Qualitative Research Symposium, January, University of Bath.

Dewey, J. (1938) *Experience and Education*, New York: Collier.

Dimeo, R. (2016) 'On inequality by Harry G. Frankfurt: A sketch note summary', *ACM SIGCAS Computers and Society*, 46(1), 6-6.

Dimeo, R. (2017) 'Sketchnote summary of "The backscattering story: A personal view"', *Journal of Neutron Research*, 19(3–4), 103–5.

Doran, G.T. (1981) 'There's a SMART way to write management's goals and objectives', *Management Review*, 70(11), 35–6.

Duckworth, A. (2017) *Grit: Why Passion and Resilience are the Secrets to Success*, London: Vermilion.

Dweck, C. (2017) *Mindset: Changing the Way You Think to Fulfil Your Potential*, New York: Robinson.

Eccleston, C. (2016) *Embodied: The Psychology of Physical Sensation*, Oxford: Oxford University Press.

Ellingson, L.L. (2009) *Engaging Crystallization in Qualitative Research: An Introduction*, London: SAGE Publications Ltd.

Ellingson, L.L. (2017) *Embodiment in Qualitative Research*, Abingdon: Routledge.

Ellingson, L.L. and Sotirin, P. (2020) *Making Data in Qualitative Research: Engagements, Ethics, and Entanglements*, Abingdon: Routledge.

Ellis, C. (2007) 'Telling secrets, revealing lives: Relational ethics in research with intimate others', *Qualitative Inquiry*, 13(1), 3–29.

Emerson, R.M., Fretz, R.I. and Shaw, L.L. (2011) *Writing Ethnographic Fieldnotes* (2nd edn), Chicago, IL: The University of Chicago Press.

Erb, V. (2012) 'How to start sketchnoting', *Bulletin of the American Society for Information Science and Technology*, 39(1), 22–3.

Etherington, K. (2004) *Becoming a Reflexive Researcher: Using Our Selves in Research*, London: Jessica Kingsley Publishers.

Faulkner, S.L. (2017) 'Poetic Inquiry', in P. Leavy (ed) *Handbook of Arts-Based Research*, New York: The Guilford Press, 208–30.

Faulkner, S.L. (2019) *Poetic Inquiry: Craft, Method and Practice*, Abingdon: Routledge.

Fernández-Fontecha, A., O'Halloran, K.L., Tan, S. and Wignell, P. (2019) 'A multimodal approach to visual thinking: The scientific sketchnote', *Visual Communication*, 18(1), 5–29.

Finlay, L. (2015) 'Sensing and making sense: Embodying metaphor in relational-centered psychotherapy', *The Humanistic Psychologist*, 43(4), 338–53.

Fluk, L.R. (2009) 'The narrative of research as a tool of pedagogy and assessment: A literature review', *Transit: The LaGuardia Journal on Teaching and Learning*, 4, 40–56.

Fluk, L.R. (2015) 'Foregrounding the research log in information literacy instruction', *The Journal of Academic Librarianship*, 41(4), 488–98.

Foley, D.E. (2002) 'Critical ethnography: The reflexive turn', *International Journal of Qualitative Studies in Education*, 15(4), 469–90.

Fook, J., White, S. and Gardner, F. (2006) 'Critical Reflection: A Review of Contemporary Literature and Understandings', in S. White, J. Fook and F. Gardner (eds) *Critical Reflection in Health and Social Care*, Maidenhead: Open University Press/McGraw-Hill, 3–10.

Foot, R., Crowe, A.R., Tollafield, K.A. and Allan, C.E. (2014) 'Exploring doctoral student identity development using a self-study approach', *Teaching and Learning Inquiry*, 2(1), 103–18.

Forrester, M.A. and Sullivan, C. (eds) (2018) *Doing Qualitative Research in Psychology: A Practical Guide*, London: SAGE Publications Ltd.

Friedemann, M.L., Mayorga, C. and Jimenez, L.D. (2011) 'Data collectors' field journals as tools for research', *Journal of Research in Nursing*, 16(5), 453–65.

Fry, S. (2006) *The Ode Less Travelled: Unlocking the Poet Within*, Harmondsworth: Penguin.

Gadd, E., Oppenheim, C. and Probets, S. (2003a) 'RoMEO Studies 1: The impact of copyright ownership on academic author self-archiving', *Journal of Documentation*, 59(3), 243–77.

Gadd, E., Oppenheim, C. and Probets, S. (2003b) 'RoMEO Studies 2: How academics want to protect their open-access research papers', *Journal of Information Science*, 29(5), 333–56.

Gadd, E., Oppenheim, C. and Probets, S. (2003c) 'RoMEO Studies 3: How academics expect to use open access research papers', *Journal of Librarianship and Information Science*, 35(3), 171–87.

Gaillet-De Chezelles, F. (2010) 'Wordsworth, a wandering poet: Walking and poetic creation', *Etudes Anglaises*, 63(1), 18–33.

Gaiman, N. (2018) 'Write down everything that happens in the story, and then in your second draft make it look like you knew what you were doing all along' [Tweet, @neilhimself], Twitter, 30 January. Available at: https://twitter.com/neilhimself/status/958449061417439233

Gann, M.N. (2002) *Targets for Tomorrow's Schools: A Guide to Whole School Target-Setting for Governors and Headteachers*, London: Routledge.

Gardner, B., Lally, P. and Wardle, J. (2012) 'Making health habitual: The psychology of "habit-formation" and general practice', *British Journal of General Practice*, 62(605), 664–6.

Gibbs, G. (1988) *Learning by Doing: A Guide to Teaching and Learning Methods*, Oxford: Further Education Unit, Oxford Brookes University.

Gibson, D. (2018) 'A visual conversation with trauma: Visual journaling in art therapy to combat vicarious trauma', *Art Therapy*, 35(2), 99–103.

Giddens, A. (1991) *Modernity and Self-Identity: Self and Society in the Late Modern Age*, Redwood City, CA: Stanford University Press.

Goffman, A. (2015) *On The Run: Fugitive Life in an American City*, London: Picador.

Gros, F. (2014) *A Philosophy of Walking*, trans J. Howe, London and New York: Verso.

Guillemin, M. and Gillam, L. (2004) 'Ethics, reflexivity, and "ethically important moments" in research', *Qualitative Inquiry*, 10(2), 261–80.

Gullion, J.S. (2014) *October Birds: A Novel about Pandemic Influenza, Infection Control and First Responders*, Rotterdam: Sense Publishers.

Hahn, C. (2008) *Doing Qualitative Research Using Your Computer: A Practical Guide*, London: SAGE Publications Ltd.

Hall, D. (2009) 'How "smart" are targets?', *HR Bulletin: Research and Practice*, 4, 8–10.

Hall, L. and Burns, L. (2009) 'Identity development and mentoring in doctoral education', *Harvard Educational Review*, 79(1), 49–70.

Hampton, S.E. and Morrow, C. (2003) 'Reflective journaling and assessment', *Journal of Professional Issues in Engineering Education and Practice*, 129(4), 186–9.

Hannula, M.S. (2003) 'Fictionalising experiences: Experiencing through fiction', *For the Learning of Mathematics*, 23(3), 31–7.

Hatch, J.A. (2002) *Doing Qualitative Research in Education Settings*, New York: SUNY Press.

Heller, S. and Landers, R. (2014a) *Infographic Designers' Sketchbooks*, New York: Princeton Architectural Press.

Heller, S. and Landers, R. (2014b) *Raw Data: Infographic Designers' Sketchbooks*, London: Thames & Hudson.

Hensley, M.K. (2011) 'Citation management software: Features and futures', *Reference & User Services Quarterly*, 50(3), 204–8.

Herrera, C.D. (1999) 'Two arguments for "covert methods" in social research', *The British Journal of Sociology*, 50(2), 331–43.

Hiemstra, R. (2001) 'Uses and Benefits of Journal Writing', in L.M. English and M.A. Gillen (eds) *Promoting Journal Writing in Adult Education: New Directions for Adult and Continuing Education*, San Francisco, CA: Jossey-Bass, 19–26. [Summary available online from: http://citeseerx.ist.psu.edu/viewdoc/download?doi=10.1.1.463.6103&rep=rep1&type=pdf]

Hobbs, J. (2014) *Sketch Your World: Essential Techniques for Drawing on Location*, London: Apple Press.

Hockey, J. and Allen-Collinson, J. (2009) 'The sensorium at work: The sensory phenomenology of the working body', *The Sociological Review*, 57(2), 217–39.

Hughes, R. and Huby, M. (2002) 'The application of vignettes in social and nursing research', *Journal of Advanced Nursing*, 37(4), 382–6.

Hughes, R. and Huby, M. (2012) 'The construction and interpretation of vignettes in social research', *Social Work and Social Sciences Review*, 11(1), 36–51.

Humble, Á. and Radina, E. (eds) (2019) *How Qualitative Data Analysis Happens: Moving Beyond 'Themes Emerged'*, Abingdon: Routledge.

Ivey, C. and Crum, J. (2018) 'Choosing the right citation management tool: EndNote, Mendeley, RefWorks, or Zotero', *JMLA: Journal of the Medical Library Association*, 106(3), 399–403.

Jackson, A.Y. and Mazzei, L.A. (eds) (2008) *Voice in Qualitative Inquiry: Challenging Conventional, Interpretive, and Critical Conceptions in Qualitative Research*, Abingdon: Routledge.

James, A. (2013) 'Seeking the analytic imagination: Reflections on the process of interpreting qualitative data', *Qualitative Research*, 13(5), 562–77.

Jensen, J. (2017) *Write No Matter What: Advice for Academics*, Chicago, IL: The University of Chicago Press.

Jha, A. (2009) *Traditional Knowledge System in India*, New Delhi: Atlantic Publishers & Distributors.

Kara, H. (2015) *Creative Research Methods in the Social Sciences: A Practical Guide*, Bristol: Policy Press.

Kara, H. (2018) *Research Ethics in the Real World: Euro-Western and Indigenous Perspectives*, Bristol: Policy Press.

Kara, H. (2020) *Creative Research Methods: A Practical Guide*, Bristol: Policy Press.

Kelley, A., Belcourt-Dittloff, A., Belcourt, C. and Belcourt, G. (2013) 'Research ethics and indigenous communities', *American Journal of Public Health*, 103(12), 2146–52.

Kerka, S. (2002) *Journal Writing as an Adult Learning Tool*, Practice Application Brief No 22, ERIC Clearinghouse on Adult, Career, and Vocational Education, Center on Education and Training for Employment, College of Education, Ohio State University. Available at: https://files.eric.ed.gov/fulltext/ED470782.pdf

King, S. (2000) *On Writing: A Memoir of the Craft*, New York: Simon & Schuster.

Kolb, D.A. (1984) *Experiential Learning: Experience as the Source of Learning and Development*, Englewood Cliffs, NJ: Prentice Hall.

Lacy, M. and Chen, H.L. (2013) 'Rethinking library instruction: Using learning-outcome based design to teach online search strategies', *Journal of Information Literacy*, 7(2), 126–48.

Lakoff, G. and Johnson, M. (2003) *Metaphors We Live By*, Chicago, IL: The University of Chicago Press.

Lally, P., van Jaarsveld, C.H., Potts, H.W. and Wardle, J. (2010) 'How are habits formed: Modelling habit formation in the real world', *European Journal of Social Psychology*, 40(6), 998–1009.

Lambourne, K. and Tomporowski, P. (2010) 'The effect of exercise-induced arousal on cognitive task performance: A meta-regression analysis', *Brain Research*, 1341, 12–24.

Lamott, A. (2020) *Bird by Bird: Instructions on Writing and Life*, Edinburgh: Canongate Books.

Lapadat, J.C. (2017) 'Ethics in autoethnography and collaborative autoethnography', *Qualitative Inquiry*, 23(8), 589–603.

Laporte, T. (2017) *Create Your Life Book: Mixed-Media Art Projects for Expanding Creativity and Encouraging Personal Growth*, Beverly, MA: Quarry Books.

Lawson, H. (1985) *Reflexivity: The Postmodern Predicament*, La Salle, IL: Open Court.

Leavy, P. (2015) *Method Meets Art: Arts-Based Research Practice* (2nd edn), New York: The Guilford Press.

Leavy, P. (2016) *Fiction as Research Practice: Short Stories, Novellas, and Novels*, Abingdon: Routledge.

Leavy, P. (2020a) *Candy Floss Collection: 3 Novels*, Rotterdam: Sense Publishers.

Leavy, P. (2020b) *Method Meets Art: Arts-Based Research Practice* (3rd edn), New York: The Guilford Press.

Lebo, M.J. (2016) 'Managing your research pipeline', *PS, Political Science & Politics*, 49(2), 259–64. Available at: https://politicalscience.uwo.ca/faculty/lebo/img/journal_pdfs/Pipeline%20PS.pdf

LeGuin, U. (1981) *The Left Hand of Darkness*, London: Orbit.

Leigh, J.S. and Brown, N. (2021) *Embodied Inquiry: Research Methods*, London: Bloomsbury.

Lejeune, P. (2009) *On Diary*, Honolulu, HI: University of Hawai'i Press.

Lieberman, A. (1987) *Documenting Professional Practice: The Vignette as a Qualitative Tool*. Available at: https://files.eric.ed.gov/fulltext/ED287866.pdf

Lindahl, C. (2018) 'Dream some more: Storytelling as therapy', *Folklore*, 129(3), 221–36.

Ludwig, L.K. (2011a) *True Vision: Authentic Art Journaling*, Beverly, MA: Quarry Books.

Ludwig, L.K. (2011b) *Creative Wildfire: An Introduction to Art Journaling – Basics and Beyond*, Beverly, MA: Quarry Books.

Lyon, D. (2016) 'Doing audio-visual montage to explore time and space: The everyday rhythms of Billingsgate Fish Market', *Sociological Research Online*, 21(3), 12. Available at: www.socresonline.org.uk/21/3/12.html

MacLure, M. (1993) 'Arguing for your self: Identity as an organising principle in teachers' jobs and lives', *British Educational Research Journal*, 19(4), 311–22.

MacLure, M. (2011) 'Qualitative inquiry: Where are the ruins?', *Qualitative Inquiry*, 17(10), 997–1005.

Maharaj, N. (2016) 'Using field notes to facilitate critical reflection', *Reflective Practice*, 17(2), 114–24.

Malinowski, B. (1961) *Argonauts of the Western Pacific*, New York: Dutton.

Marino, W. (2012) 'Fore-cite: Tactics for evaluating citation management tools', *Reference Services Review*, 40(2), 295–310.

Marx, K. (1932) *Economic and Philosophic Manuscripts of 1844*, New Delhi: Progress Publishers. Available at: www.marxists.org/archive/marx/works/1844/manuscripts/preface.htm

Maurizio, L. (1995) 'Anthropology and spirit possession: A reconsideration of the Pythia's role at Delphi', *The Journal of Hellenic Studies*, 115, 69–86.

May, T. and Perry, B. (2017) *Reflexivity: The Essential Guide*, London: SAGE Publications Ltd.

Mena-Marcos, J., García-Rodríguez, M.L. and Tillema, H. (2013) 'Student teacher reflective writing: What does it reveal?', *European Journal of Teacher Education*, 36(2), 147–63.

Miller, R.W. (2017) *How to Bullet Plan: Everything You Need to Know about Journaling with Bullet Points*, London: Pan Macmillan.

Moon, J.A. (2006) *Learning Journals: A Handbook for Reflective Practice and Professional Development* (2nd edn), Abingdon: Routledge.

Morgan, D.L. (2018) 'Themes, theories, and models', *Qualitative Health Research*, 28(3), 339–45.

Morton, J. and Storch, N. (2019) 'Developing an authorial voice in PhD multilingual student writing: The reader's perspective', *Journal of Second Language Writing*, 43, 15–23.

Nelson, N. and Castelló, M. (2012) 'Academic Writing and Authorial Voice', in M. Castelló and C. Donahue (eds) *University Writing: Selves and Texts in Academic Societies*, Bingley: Emerald, 33–51.

Nelson, R. (2013) *Practice as Research in the Arts: Principles, Protocols, Pedagogies, Resistances*, Basingstoke: Palgrave Macmillan.

Nolas, S.M. and Varvantakis, C. (2019) 'Field notes for amateurs', *Social Analysis*, 63(3), 130–48.

O'Mara, S. (2020) *In Praise of Walking: The New Science of How We Walk and Why It's Good for Us*, London: Vintage.

Oppezzo, M. and Schwartz, D.L. (2014) 'Give your ideas some legs: The positive effect of walking on creative thinking', *Journal of Experimental Psychology: Learning, Memory, and Cognition*, 40(4), 1142–52.

Overall, S. (2021) *walk write (repeat)*, Axminster: Triarchy Press.

Pacheco-Vega, R. (2019) 'Writing field notes and using them to prompt scholarly writing', *International Journal of Qualitative Methods*, 18, 1–2.

Parker, T.S. and Wampler, K.S. (2006) 'Changing emotion: The use of therapeutic storytelling', *Journal of Marital and Family Therapy*, 32(2), 155–66.

Phillippi, J. and Lauderdale, J. (2018) 'A guide to field notes for qualitative research: Context and conversation', *Qualitative Health Research*, 28(3), 381–8.

Phillips, R. and Kara, H. (2021) *Creative Writing for Social Research: A Practical Guide*, Bristol: Policy Press.

Pillow, W. (2003) 'Confession, catharsis, or cure? Rethinking the uses of reflexivity as methodological power in qualitative research', *International Journal of Qualitative Studies in Education*, 16(2), 175–96.

Prendergast, M. (2009) '"Poem is what?" Poetic inquiry in qualitative social science research', *International Review of Qualitative Research*, 1(4), 541–68.

Prendergast, M., Leggo, C. and Sameshima, P. (eds) (2009) *Poetic Inquiry: Vibrant Voices in the Social Sciences*, Rotterdam: Sense Publishers.

Pullman, P. (2021) *Dæmon Voices: On Stories and Storytelling*, edited by Simon Mason, Oxford: David Fickling Books.

Ramcharan, P. and Cutcliffe, J.R. (2001) 'Judging the ethics of qualitative research: Considering the "ethics as process" model', *Health & Social Care in the Community*, 9(6), 358–66.

Rapport, N. (1991) 'Writing fieldnotes: The conventionalities of note-taking and taking note in the field', *Anthropology Today*, 7(1), 10–13.

Ray, A.K. and Ramesh, D.B. (2017) 'Zotero: Open source citation management tool for researchers', *International Journal of Library and Information Sciences*, 7(3), 238–45.

Renold, E. (2002) 'Using vignettes in qualitative research', *Building Research Capacity*, 3–5.

Richardson, L. (2000) 'Writing: A Method of Inquiry', in N. Denzin and Y. Lincoln (eds) *The SAGE Handbook of Qualitative Research* (2nd edn), Thousand Oaks, CA: SAGE Publications Ltd, 923–43.

Richardson, L. (2003) 'Writing: A Method of Inquiry', in Y. Lincoln and N. Denzin (eds) *Turning Points in Qualitative Research: Tying Knots in a Handkerchief*, Walnut Creek, CA: Altamira, 379–96.

Richman, J. and Mercer, D. (2002) 'The vignette revisited: Evil and the forensic nurse', *Nurse Researcher*, 9, 70–82.

Rogers, R.R. (2001) 'Reflection in higher education: A concept analysis', *Innovative Higher Education*, 26(1), 37–57.

Rohde, M. (2013) *The Sketchnote Handbook: The Illustrated Guide to Visual Note Taking*, San Francisco, CA: Peachpit Press.

Rolfe, G., Freshwater, D. and Jasper, M. (2001) *Critical Reflection in Nursing and the Helping Professions: A User's Guide*, Basingstoke: Palgrave Macmillan.

Ronis, D.L., Yates, J.F. and Kirscht, J.P. (1988) 'Attitudes, Decisions, and Habits as Determinants of Repeated Behavior', in A.R. Pratkanis, S.J. Breckler and A.G. Greenwald (eds) *Attitude Structure and Function*, 213–39.

Rose, G. (2016) *Visual Methodologies: An Introduction to Researching with Visual Materials* (4th edn), London: SAGE Publications Ltd.

Rosen, M. (2012) *Fantastic Mr Dahl*, Harmondsworth: Penguin.

Roth, W.M. (2009) 'Auto/ethnography and the question of ethics', *Forum Qualitative Sozialforschung/Forum: Qualitative Social Research*, 10(1), Article 38.

Rubin, J.A. (ed) (2016) *Approaches to Art Therapy: Theory and Technique*, Abingdon: Routledge.

Sala-Bubaré, A. and Castelló, M. (2017) 'Exploring the relationship between doctoral students' experiences and research community positioning', *Studies in Continuing Education*, 39(1), 16–34.

Scarry, E. (1985) *The Body in Pain: The Making and Unmaking of the World*, Oxford: Oxford University Press.

Schön, D.A. (1987) *Educating the Reflective Practitioner: Towards a New Design for Teaching in the Professions*, San Francisco, CA: Jossey-Bass.

Shaw, I.G.R. and Holland, S. (2014) *Doing Qualitative Research in Social Work*, London: SAGE Publications Ltd.

Silverman, D. (2017) *Doing Qualitative Research* (5th edn), London: SAGE Publications Ltd.

Skilling, K. and Stylianides, G.J. (2020) 'Using vignettes in educational research: A framework for vignette construction', *International Journal of Research & Method in Education*, 43(5), 541–56.

Skinner, C.H., Rhymer, K.N. and McDaniel, E.C. (2000) 'Naturalistic Direct Observation in Educational Settings', in E.S. Shapiro and T.R. Kratochwill (eds) *Conducting School-Based Assessments of Child and Adolescent Behavior*, The Guilford School Practitioner Series, New York: The Guilford Press, 21–54.

Smith, H. and Dean, R.T. (eds) (2009) *Practice-Led Research, Research-Led Practice in the Creative Arts*, Edinburgh: Edinburgh University Press.

Smith, J.A., Flowers, P. and Larkin, M. (2012) *Interpretative Phenomenological Analysis: Theory, Method and Research*, London: SAGE Publications Ltd.

Smith, S. (2006) 'Encouraging the use of reflexivity in the writing up of qualitative research', *International Journal of Therapy and Rehabilitation*, 13(5), 209–15.

Sontag, S. (2003) *Regarding the Pain of Others*, London: Penguin Books.

Sontag, S. (2012) *Reborn: Early Diaries 1947–1963*, London: Penguin Books.

Sorger, R. and Udale, J. (2017) *The Fundamentals of Fashion Design*, London: Bloomsbury Publishing.

Sotirin, P. (2010) 'Autoethnographic mother-writing: Advocating radical specificity', *Journal of Research Practice*, 6(1), M9.

Stevens, D.D. and Cooper, J.E. (2009) *Journal Keeping: How to Use Reflective Writing for Learning, Teaching, Professional Insight and Positive Change*, Sterling, VA: Stylus Publications.

Stewart, R. (2010) 'Creating New Stories for Praxis: Navigations, Narrations, Neonarratives', in E. Barrett and B. Bolt (eds) *Practice as Research: Approaches to Creative Arts Enquiry*, London: Bloomsbury, 123–33.

Syed, M. (2015) *Black Box Thinking: The Surprising Truth About Success*, Harmondsworth: Penguin.

Tamas, S. (2009) 'Writing and righting trauma: Troubling the autoethnographic voice', *Forum Qualitative Sozialforschung/Forum: Qualitative Social Research*, 10(1), Article 22.

Thanssoulis, E. (1999) 'Setting achievement targets for school children', *Education Economics*, 7(2), 101–19.

Thomas, D.S.M. (1998) 'The use of portfolio learning in medical education', *Medical Teacher*, 20(3), 192–9.

Thompson, N. and Pascal, J. (2012) 'Developing critically reflective practice', *Reflective Practice*, 13(2), 311–25.

Thorpe, K. (2004) 'Reflective learning journals: From concept to practice', *Reflective Practice*, 5(3), 327–43.

Toom, A., Husu, J. and Patrikainen, S. (2015) 'Student teachers' patterns of reflection in the context of teaching practice', *European Journal of Teacher Education*, 38(3), 320–40.

Tripp, D. (1993) *Critical Incidents in Teaching: Developing Professional Judgement*, London: Routledge.

Viete, R. and Ha, P.L. (2007) 'The growth of voice: Expanding possibilities for representing self in research writing', *English Teaching: Practice and Critique*, 6(2), 39–57.

Walford, G. (2009) 'The practice of writing ethnographic fieldnotes', *Ethnography and Education*, 4(2), 117–30.

Watson, D. (2010) 'Teaching teachers to think: Reflective journaling as a strategy to enhance students understanding and practice of academic writing', *Journal of College Teaching & Learning*, 7(12), 11–18.

Werle Lee, K.P. (2010) 'Planning for success: Setting SMART goals for study', *British Journal of Midwifery*, 18(11), 744–6.

Wolf, K. (1996) 'Developing an effective teaching portfolio', *Educational Leadership*, 53(6), 34–7.

Wolfinger, N.H. (2002) 'On writing fieldnotes: Collection strategies and background expectancies', *Qualitative Research*, 2(1), 85–93.

Woodward, S. (2019) *Material Methods: Researching and Thinking with Things*, London: SAGE Publications Ltd.

Yiannouli, A. (2019) 'The point of a bullet journal', *The Veterinary Record*, 185(6), 180.

References

Yoon, K.S., Garet, M., Birman, B. and Jacobson, R. (2007) *Examining the Effects of Mathematics and Science Professional Development on Teachers' Instructional Practice: Using Professional Development Activity Log*, Mathematics Science Partnership Professional Development Evaluation Report, Washington, DC: Council of Chief State School Officers, American Institutes for Research.

Index

References to figures are in *italic* type

A

academic integrity 79, 102
achievements, recording 35
Ackerman, Lauren 33–4, *34*
acrylics 16
Ancient Rome 5
annotations *68*, 68–9, 75
anonymity 84, 87
appearance of research journals 9–24
    bindings and covers 12–13
    choosing one 11–14
    colours and textures 15–17
    electronic journals 17–21
    format and size 11–12
    page patterns 14
    paper weight 13–14
    writing tools 14–16
arts-based approach 7, 21, *22*, 52–5,
    54, 74
    materials 15–17
assemblages 55
Atkinson, Paul 78
audio recordings 17, 18, 55–9, 67,
    84
authenticity 73–4
autoethnography 21, 84, 102–3

B

bibliographies 19–20, 68
bindings and covers 12–13
blogs 20–1, 24, 55
Boroditsky, Lera 100
Brill Sense Publishers 88
Brookfield, Stephen 47
brushes 16
bullet journals 8, 30
Burgess, Robert 78
business cards 29

C

cameras 58–9
CaMLISd template 27
Candy Floss Collection 88
choosing what to record 67–74
coding 80–1, 93
collages 17
colours and textures 15–17
computer programs and applications
    18–20
confidentiality 87, 102
consent 102, 103
content and scope 25–43
    to-do lists 29–30
    journalling from the field 35–7
    note-taking 26–8
    trackers 30–5, *31*, *32*
Cornell, Joseph 55
covers 12–13
COVID-19 pandemic 88–91,
    90–1
creative thinking 65, 66–7
critical incidents 69–73, *70–2*, 74,
    75
criticality 81
crochet 53
cross-referencing 68–9
CUTE targets 30–1
CVs 35

D

Danêk, Clare 21, *22*
data protection 57
Delamont, Sara 82
Dewey, John 5
dictaphones 57, 67
digital audio recorders 57–8
digital cameras 58–9

dissemination 83–92, 93–4
  fictionalisation 87–91, *90–1*
  graphic novels 84–7, *85–6*

E
electronic journals 17–21
Ellis, Carolyn 103–4
Embodied Inquiry 52–5
Emerson, Robert 73–4
emotional baggage/dumping 82–3, 84, 93
emotions and experiences 36–7, 46, 51
EndNote 19, 20
ethics 84, 87, 101–4
ethnography 43–4, 73, 102–3
ethnopoetics 48–9, *48*
Evernote 19
evidence, journal entries as 78–9
exercising 66–7

F
Facebook 20
fictionalisation 47–9
  dissemination 87–91, *90–1*
fieldnotes 10, 35–7, 43–4, 73–4
finance trackers 31–3, *32*
Fluk, Louise 6–7
format and size of journal 11–12
Fry, Stephen 49

G
Gaiman, Neil 90
Gibbs, Graham 46–7
Goffman, Alice 103
Google Keep 19
GoPro cameras 59
graphic novels 84–7, *85–6*
Greene, Graham 17–18
Gullion, Jessica Smartt 88

H
habits 62–3
Höch, Hannah 55

I
ideas tracker 34
identity 104–5
immediacy 73–4
index 21
Instagram 20, 42
internet searches 41–2
Interpretative Phenomenological
    Analysis 80

J
Jensen, Joli 82–3
jottings 73
journalling, concept of 4–6
  key messages 108–9
  research journalling 6–8
journalling from the field 35–7, 64–5
junk journals 23–4

K
Kara, Helen 64
knitting 53, *54*
knowledge, traditional 101
Kuuk Thaayorre language 100

L
language, and sensory experiences
    100
Leavy, Patricia 52–3, 88
Lieberman, Ann *70*
lists 29–30, *39*
literary devices 47–9, 87–91
living the research process 40
logs 3, 5–7
London School of Hygiene and Tropical
    Medicine *45*, 45–6
Lyon, Dawn 60

M
marker pens 15
Marx, Karl 99
McAllister, Aine *48*, 48–9, 107,
    108

Mendeley 19, 20
methodological account 78–9
microphones 57
Microsoft OneNote 19
mind maps 27–8
mini-journals 23
misconduct, academic 79
mixed-media tools 17
mobile apps 20
mobile phones 56–7, 67
models of reflection 46–7, 55
mood blankets 53

N
note-taking 26–8
    annotations 68–9, *68*, 75
    fieldnotes 10, 35–7, 43–4, 73–4
    software 19
    templates 44–6

O
observation templates *45*, 45–6
observations and conversations, 36–7,
    55–6, 68
O'Mara, Shane 67
OneNote 19
online research journals 24
Overall, Sonia 67

P
Pacheco-Vega, Raul 38–9, *38–9*
page patterns 14
paints/paintings 16, 53–4
paper
    junk journals 23–4
    page patterns 14
    sizes 11–12
    weight of 13–14
pastels 16
pedagogy 104–6
pencils 15–16
pens 15
photography 56, 58–9
photomontage 55

Pinterest 20, 42
playing with words 50–2, *50–1*
podcasts 20–1
poetic inquiry 47–9, *48*
Practice As Research 98–9
Price, Lesley *31*, 68–9, *68*, 80
procedural ethics 102
process of journalling 43–60
    arts-based approach 52–5
    fictionalisation and poetic inquiry
        47–9, *48*
    playing with words 50–2, *50–1*
    reflective models 46–7
    technology 55–9
    templates 44–6
project management 33–4, *34*

Q
quilting 54

R
recording information (audio/video)
    55–9, 84
referencing software and applications
    19–20
reflective models 46–7
reflexivity 35–6, 64–5, 81–2
RefWorks 19, 20
relational ethics 102–3
research journals (overview) 3–8
    concept of journalling 4–6
    concept of research journalling
        6–8
research pipeline 33–4, *34*
researcher wellbeing 82–3
Ringgold, Faith 53–4
Romans 5

S
scenarios 69–73
scheduling times 63–5
    unscheduled opportunities 65–7
sense-making 79–83
senses 41, 60, 99–100

situational ethics 102
size of journal 11–12
sketchnotes 27–8, *28*
SMART targets 30–1
smartphones 56–7, 67
Social Fictions Series 88
social media 20–1, 24, 55–6, 102
software 18–20
Sontag, Susan 109
soundscapes 57, 84
Squarespace 20
stitch journal 21, *22*

T
tablets 56–7
targets 30–1, *31*
teaching 104–6
technology 17–21, 55–9
templates 44–6, *70*, *72*
text documents (electronic) 17–18
theoretical frameworks 96–101
think-walks 66–7, 75–6
thoughts and reflections 36, 37
timing 61–76
    choosing what to record 67–74
    critical incidents and vignettes
        69–73, *70–2*, 74, 75
    habits 62–3
    immediacy and authenticity 73–4
    notes and annotations 68–9, *68*,
        75
    scheduling 63–5
    unscheduled opportunities 65–7
    walking 66–7
to-do lists 29–30, *39*
trackers 30–5, *31*, *32*
traditional knowledge 101
transparency 81
Twitter 20

U
unscheduled opportunities 65–7
using journal entries 77–94
    analysis 80–1, 93
    cyclical nature of 92

dissemination 83–92, 93–4
    as evidence 78–9
    graphic novels 84–7, *85–6*
    reflexivity 81–2
    researcher wellbeing 82–3
    sense-making 79–83

V
video recordings 20, 55–60, 84
vignettes 69–73, *70–2*, 75
Vimeo 20
visual note-taking 27–8
vlogs 20–1
voice (researcher) 104–5

W
walking 66–7, 75–6
watercolours 16
websites 20, 24
weight of paper 13–14
wellbeing 82–3
WhatsApp 56, 102
White, Madeline 53, *54*
Wilde, Oscar 80
Wix 20
Word 20
word clouds 51–2
WordPress 20
Wordsworth, William 66
Wragg, Jason 84–7, *85–6*
writing
    fictionalisation 47–9, 87–91,
        90–1
    voice and identity 104–5
writing tools 14–16
Wunderlist 19

Y
YouTube 20

Z
Zoom audio recorders 58
Zotero 19, 20

Printed and bound by CPI Group (UK) Ltd, Croydon, CR0 4YY

25/03/2025

14647336-0005